What readers are saying about
Some Leaders Are Born Women!

"*Some Leaders Are Born Women!* is full of inspiring stories, practical strategies, and valuable advice from thirty-seven highly successful female leaders. It will inspire and motivate you to find and express your own inner leader more fully."

— Jack Canfield, co-author of *Chicken Soup for the Woman's Soul* and *Chicken Soup for the Soul at Work*

"This wonderful book provides instant inspiration on every page! Each essay is a story of courage from women who are the backbone of their companies, communities, and families. I'm keeping the book in easy reach for when I need a quick dose of encouragement."

— Ardath Rodale, chairman, Rodale Inc.

"Joan Gustafson has created a leadership primer—a rich compilation of teaching tales designed to instruct and inspire. The reader finds herself caught in a powerful web of women's lives, moving along the paths set by businesswomen, mothers, writers and teachers, while learning what constitutes leadership, how it can be cultivated and what rewards are reaped when women live from their core of natural feminine power. *Some Leaders are Born Women!* belongs on the 'required reading' lists of high schools and colleges across America, and at the bedsides of women who still need reminding that each of us is a born leader. Thank you, Joan."

— Kathleen Calabrese, Ph.D.

"When women become leaders, it takes a lot of effort not to give up. Joan Gustafson's book is an inspiring collection of advice imparted by wise women. This is networking at its best within the pages of one book."

— Lillian Vernon, founder and chief executive officer, Lillian Vernon Corporation

"Charismatic leaders are likely born that way. Most leaders, however, learn from experience and the lessons of others, combined with their own unique intuition to find the leader within. *Some Leaders Are Born Women* shares with us the way many successful women have turned themselves into a new breed of leaders. These are real-life women, not textbook fare. Read, learn, and enjoy. There is a wealth of wisdom here."

—Constance B. Wolf, president, Sounding Board

"The influence of good women is needed now more than ever before. As women, let us rise to the challenge and lead those around us to finding solutions and standing and defending those things that women naturally hold dear—freedom, family and friends. The example of the women in *Some Leaders Are Born Women!* gives us the courage to rise to our potential and make a difference."

—Colleen Down, author, *It Takes a Mother to Raise a Village*

"Some leaders are born women, and some writers are born leaders. Joan Gustafson has done it again! Her magnetic personality brings together an outstanding group of women leaders to follow her vision of giving them a stage, to express their philosophies and experiences about this very important subject—leadership. This book is an insightful collection of real life experiences that every young lady starting her first steps into the most competitive world should read. As for the men of the world, as they learn from this fabulous state-of-the-art document, it will change their way of looking at us."

—Sara Arbel, founder and president, Coach-In,
Tel Aviv, Israel

"Absolutely awesome! The advice and strategies outlined by each of these dynamic female leaders are incredibly insightful. Joan, you have created a legacy of learning on what leadership is all about. This book, though it is geared towards women, can help both genders develop the leader within."

—Mark Smith, president and founder, Cocoon Creations, Inc.

"*Some Leaders are Born Women!* is an outstanding treatment—insightful and swift reading—packed with pearls from leaders who've walked the talk—on the all-important subject of effective leadership. No matter your gender or your current position, this book supplies a trove of 'how to's and why's' that will fuel your leadership growth."

—Dr. Dennis R. Deaton, founder and chairman,
Quma Learning, Inc.

"I highly recommend *Some Leaders Are Born Women!* I would say most women are born leaders. Females seem to have inbred leadership qualities that allow them to succeed in the most challenging circumstances. It is the feminine qualities that is most lacking in leadership today. As more and more women discover and exert their leadership abilities, we will have far better leadership in the world."

—Dean R. Portinga, Th.D., Ph.D. creator of the Unlimited Futures, Spiritual Insights Programs, director, Life Science Foundation

"For any woman wanting life-changing, powerful support to rise to the next level of leadership in her life, this book provides an inspiring and practical roadmap to becoming a leader through uplifting real-life stories, invaluable tips, and clearly defined leadership qualities."

—Andrea Epel Lieberstein, MPH, R.D.

"Some leaders *are* born women! The stories these women leaders tell are truly inspiring. Their lives are shining examples to all women, and the message that all women are leaders needs to be heard. Now, more than ever, we need to see and hear powerful women. Government, education, community, and business must be influenced by women to make the world a better place. The lessons and advice in *Some Leaders Are Born Women!* will surely motivate the leader waiting in all of us."

—Linda M. Herold, founder and president, Herold Enterprises

"Joan Gustafson's latest book frames powerful stories from a broad spectrum of leaders-born-women, within seven sound leadership practices. Catalytic and timely!"

—Laraine Rodgers, president, Arizona Partnership for Higher Education and Business

"America is the birthplace of the modern women's movement and it shows in *Some Leaders Are Born Women!* Wave after wave of successful, intelligent women splash onto the pages of Joan Gustafson's new book. I couldn't put it down!"

—Deborah Cartstens, women's political advocate, The WISH List, The White House Project

"If this is a woman's book, I want to be a woman! Joan Gustafson has managed to compile an incredible 'chicken soup' of business leadership and wisdom. Each short chapter provides an easy-to-read nugget of knowledge. I wanted to devour the entire pot in one sitting, but realized savoring each nugget, one at a time, was enough to keep me inspirationally fed all day!"

—Dr. Michael R. Norwood, author of *The 9 Insights of the Wealthy Soul* and the *Wealthier Weekly* newsletter (www.wealthysoul.com)

"Success doesn't just fall into your lap. Sometimes women have to stumble and pick themselves up before they realize their full potential. Joan Gustafson has compiled stories of winners of all walks of life and showcased them in her new book. Compelling!"

—Karen Carter, CLU, Ch.F.C.

"Women in business just can't get enough tools for leadership. Remember; we are still behind chronologically, in the business world. Joan Gustafson will help us all catch up."

—Jean Hollands, CEO, Growth & Leadership Center, Mountain View, California

"*Some Leaders Are Born Women!* is a powerful, intimate collection of personal and professional stories of women in leadership positions, profiling how they got there and the attributes that ultimately led to their success, in their own words. It is both compelling and inspirational—a true testament to those who broke through the glass ceiling, and the rest of us, who now stand on their shoulders, peering into the future in business, government and our private lives. My thanks to Joan Gustafson for this insightful look into such rich and courageous lives!"

—Victoria Harker, chief financial officer and vice president of Operations and Information Technology, MCI

"It was a real pleasure to read this book, and I found it hard to put down. Reading about women, successful women, is hugely motivating and fascinating, because there is something I recognize in each woman's story—something heartfelt, real, and down-to-earth. Joan Gustafson has woven these stories into a book that is easily readable and interesting. It encourages women to think: 'Oh, perhaps I'm a leader, too.'"

—Maggie Rogers, CEO, Online Center of Excellence, London, England

"*Some Leaders Are Born Women!* is a fun read. You can pick it up and have a helpful conversation with a successful woman at any time of the day."
   —Debra Benton, author, *How to Think Like a CEO*

"With Joan Gustafson's guidance and insight, we learn the core attitudes necessary to becoming a leader. *Some Leaders Are Born Women!* breaks down the mechanics of *how* this happens in clear, concise language. Motivated by the real life stories of other women who have shared this experience, *Some Leaders Are Born Women!* paves the way for the journey toward discovering our limitless possibilities."
   —Susan Winter, relationship specialist and author,
   Older Women, Younger Men

"Joan Gustafson is an inspirational leader who brings us outstanding learnings that teach us to be more effective leaders."
   —Barbara McDuffie Kahler, Leadership in Action, CEO
   and executive coach (former IBM executive)

"In *Some Leaders Are Born Women!*, Joan Eleanor Gustafson's premise is simple—women are born leaders. For this birthright to be fulfilled, ordinary women must triumph over adversity, harness unbounded energy, and use laser focused purpose to achieve extraordinary success. How does this happen? In each vignette, a woman speaks of the qualities that have made her the leader she is today. Qualities of openheartedness, dedication, courage, generosity, and integrity feature prominently in these inspirational autobiographical stories. This book is a must read for future women leaders eager to learn the lessons of their pioneering predecessors."
   —Steven Gans, Ph.D., managing director,
   Online Center of Excellence

"In knowing Joan Gustafson, I have become aware that the wide range of truths in this book live within her. I am moved and awed by the magnitude of awareness, the depths of journeys, and the breadth of accomplishments in these pages. May you take these words and experiences to your heart and let them live within you, as ever-glowing embers, so they kindle your own inner leader, inspiring you to continue to bring to life what you visualize for your world. Know in your heart that you are truly magnificent."
   —Barbara Goodman, *Inspiring the Greatness in Others*

"I absolutely love the title and stories in Joan Gustafson's book! *Some Leaders Are Born Women!* is a motivating collection of stories that women can easily relate to. It assists women to not only recognize their own leadership qualities, but how to translate them into their personal situations to create desired results in their lives."
—Charleen Tajiri, founder and CEO, VisionHealth

"Joan Gustafson, as to be expected, has come out with another winning, inspirational book. It is a must read!"
—Lois Joy Crandell Hofmann, CEO emeritus,
Genetronics, Inc.

"Joan Gustafson's newest book, *Some Leaders Are Born Women!*, piques your interest with the title alone. As with her first book about women and success, men as well as women can glean new insights for successful living. The book is a collection of essays by women in leadership positions from all walks of life. I suggest the 'one-a-day' approach—each individual contributing author has so much to offer that a day of reflection gives you a chance to react and take action. I also suggest rereading each essay at a later time to see a different perspective."
—Marilyn Straka, founder and president, On The Level

"*Some Leaders Are Born Women!* gives overviews of numerous styles of leadership. Find yourself and your special leadership abilities in the stories of the many successful women who contributed to this book. It also gives you some very important information about developing leadership qualities within yourself."
—Bobbie R. Stevens, Ph.D., president, Unlimited Futures, LLC,
author: *Unlimited Futures: How to Understand the Life You Have and Create the Life You Want*

"I'd love to give everyone I know a copy of *Some Leaders are Born Women!*, so they can feel the same motivation and inspiration I felt the first time I read the book. From the minute that I read Joan's overview, I couldn't put it down. Each woman's unique experience kept the pages turning. We really can do anything, both personally and professionally, by envisioning our dreams and creating a plan to carry them out."
—Cheryl N. Campbell, vice president,
corporate communications and public pelations,
Convergys Corporation

Some Leaders

Are

Born Women!

Some Leaders

Are

Born Women!

Stories and Strategies for Building the Leader Within You

Joan Eleanor Gustafson

Leader Dynamics

ISBN: 0-9703026-1-4 Case-bound
LCCN: 2002094182 Case-bound
ISBN: 0-9703026-2-2 Trade paperback
LCCN: 2002094461 Trade paperback

Book production by Tabby House
Cover by Aulicino Design
Front cover photo by Linda Enger Photography

Publisher's Cataloging-in-Publication
(Provided by Quality Books, Inc.)

Gustafson, Joan Eleanor
    Some leaders are born women! : stories and strategies
for building the leader within you / Joan Eleanor
Gustafson.
    p. cm.
    Includes bibliographical references and index.
    LCCN 2002094461 / (2002094182 Case-bound)
    ISBN 0-9703026-2-2 / (0-9703026-1-4 Case-bound)

    1. Leadership. 2. Leadership in women. I. Title.

BF637 .L4G87 2003   158'.4'082
                         QB102-200653

Leader Dynamics
PMB 296, Ste. A 109
3655 W. Anthem Way
Anthem, AZ 85086
publisher@leaderdynamics.com

Dedication

To my granddaughters, Alea and Erika,
who represent the next generation of female leaders

Acknowledgments

During the time I spent writing, compiling and editing *Some Leaders Are Born Women!*, I thought often about the blessings I have received throughout my life. Several additional blessings came to me through the many wonderful people who gave of their time, talents, and hearts to this book.

Thirty-seven women, who are leaders in businesses, communities and professions, contributed their stories and/or advice to help others to become more effective leaders. I am grateful to each of these women for enriching my life, as well as the lives of our readers. A special thanks to each of them: Kimberly Anderson-Maggi, Sara Arbel, Debra Benton, Patti Cain-Stanley, Dr. Kathleen Calabrese, Cheryl Campbell, Karen Carter, Lois Crandell, Leslie Dashew, Dr. Debra Davenport, Julie Davis, Colleen Down, Norma Earl, Dr. Jeanne Notto Elnadry, Barbara Goodman, Victoria Harker, Linda Herold, Jean Hollands, Beth mAcdonald, Barbara McDuffie Kahler, Gayle Anne Kelley, Dr. Audri Lanford, Andrea Lieberstein, Marion Lonn, Robin Muscia, Betty Notto, Delores Ray, Wendy Franz Richards, Ardath Rodale, Laraine Rodgers, Maggie Rogers, Dr. Bobbie Stevens, Marilyn Straka, Terry Swack, Vicki Tolman, Lillian Vernon, and Connie Wolf. To this list, I add my appreciation to Linda Chandler and Jill Lublin, who shared their stories through direct interviews.

My wonderful husband, Cliff Gustafson, has been my biggest fan, and I thank him for his support and encouragement, as well as all of the errands he ran and the delicious meals he cooked as I worked on this project.

It is with deep appreciation that I also acknowledge my editors, Carolyn Jensen and Carla Teetzel, for their diligence and attention to detail in editing the original manuscript. Thanks also to Gloria Aguirre for transcribing the interviews.

Finally, I am grateful to all leaders, both women and men, who have set examples for me during my life. By doing so, they have helped me to become a more effective leader and have contributed to each of the readers of this book.

Contents

Introduction

Some Leaders Are Born Women!

When asked why there are so few women heading Fortune 500 companies, Roselyn O'Connell, president of the National Women's Political Caucus, responded, "One word: entitlement. Men feel entitled. . . . We need to help women start to see themselves as leaders."

According to a survey by the International Labor Organization, the percentage of women holding executive management positions in the 500 largest U. S. companies has now risen to 5.1 percent. Nevertheless, many observers say that the glass ceiling remains in place. Yes, women do hold more than 5 percent of the executive positions, but women now make up more than half of the workforce.

The women featured in this book are all leaders in various areas of life—business, community, family, and charitable and social organizations. Thirty-seven of these leaders have contributed their leadership stories, insights and advice, so that readers of this book can enhance their leadership skills. In addition, information from interviews with two more leaders, Linda Chandler and Jill Lublin, is included throughout the book.

What is a leader? Although many businesspeople have used the terms *leadership* and *management* interchangeably, they are not the same. Traditional management consists of planning, budgeting, organizing, staffing, directing, and controlling. Leadership, on the other hand, consists of creating a vision; developing strategies; aligning, motivating, inspiring, and energizing people; and establishing direction. A manager produces short-term results, whereas a leader produces dramatic change. It has been said that both leaders and managers do things right, but leaders also do the right things. Although it is possible for a person to be both a manager and a leader, this book focuses on the essential characteristics for women to be leaders in today's world.

Jill Lublin, speaker and author of the international best-seller, *Guerrilla Publicity*, said, "A leader is someone who is willing to take a stand, a person who is willing to get going, regardless of how difficult things are at the moment or may be in the future. A leader keeps moving forward, and being a leader starts from the inside."

Linda Chandler, who owns four companies and is a sought-after motivational speaker, adds that we are all leaders in our own lives. "True leaders are those that create the most value in the world," she said. "They do this through the power of their ideas, the intensity of their commitment and passion, and the authenticity of their character."

During my research on characteristics, skills, and habits of female leaders, I determined that the most effective leaders shared the following seven practices:

1. **Dare to dream.** As visionaries, effective leaders see beyond the obvious. Engaging in the process of visualization, they know that they can achieve their dreams.
2. **Grow through challenge.** Each of the leaders featured in this book has overcome major challenges to become successful. They understand the importance of taking risks, and they embrace change.
3. **Set powerful goals.** Effective leaders know that they can achieve goals that others might consider impossible, and they know how to integrate their goals with their vision.
4. **Focus on the power and possibilities in people.** Understanding that people want to contribute their best efforts, effective leaders are able to accomplish more through people.

5. **Communicate effectively.** Since leadership involves getting things done through other people, effective leaders not only articulate well but they are also excellent listeners.

6. **Set high standards and live accordingly.** Integrity is of utmost importance to the best leaders, and they lead by example.

7. **Live their priorities.** Because effective leaders know and live their priorities, they are able to devote their time to those activities that are most important in their lives.

This book contains a section for each of the above practices. Starting with my experience and thoughts on the particular practice, each section contains a series of contributions from effective female leaders.

Whether you know it or not, there is a leader within you. You could be a leader in business or in medicine. You could be a leader in politics or in a civic organization. You could also be a leader in your community or in a charitable organization. Even if you choose not to lead an organization, you have it within you to be the leader within your own life and sphere of influence. Although most of the women featured in this book are business leaders, you do not have to lead a business or other type of large organization to use your leadership skills. If you are a mother, you are in an extremely important leadership role. If you are in a position where you might set an example for others, you also have the opportunity to lead.

The leaders in this book are committed to helping you to build and enhance the leader within you through experiences and advice in the following pages. May you continue to build that fantastic leader who lives within *you*!

Leading in Our Own Way

Leslie Dashew

We women are unique in how we lead
and
We must celebrate our own way.
We lead through example,
often kind and firm
or we lead through exploration, trust and openness.
We tend to be team players and enjoy the collaboration that affords.
We encourage, support and reward.
Our leadership often comes from the heart;
we draw upon our intuition as well as our smarts;
we can be passionate, especially when our values are involved;
yet we remain humble and true stewards, above all.
Our leadership is not always apparent.
Sometimes we are in the background
leading through dialogue with the actor out front on the stage.
We may be the "strength behind the throne":
an advisor, a sage.
Glory is secondary to getting the right thing done.
But we must not minimize our opportunities and
responsibilities for leadership.
We must heed the call
whether that's the call of a family member needing aid
or a business decision which must be made.

Whether it is to serve on the board
or to ask important questions and gently challenge . . .
something we may abhor.
Sometimes we must take issue with the old ways
to allow the system to grow
for we understand the seasons of life
and the importance of new growth to the continuity of
our world.
This takes courage.
This takes commitment.
This takes energy and
This takes love,
Something women leaders have an abundance of.
Our challenge is to let go of the old ways, ourselves.
To find our individual way of leading
To decide where we want to apply our energies
and to go forth with our courage, commitment, energy and love
and make our own unique contribution.
We've been doing it for millions of years.
But now there are a greater range of roles and stages
on which we can perform
And as we move through the seasons of our lives,
we can choose the focus and style of our leadership,
From being a calm presence to a dynamic force.
This is the power of a woman.

© 1999, Leslie Dashew

Section I

Dare to Dream!

Dare to Dream!

Joan Eleanor Gustafson

As a young child in Alabama in the 1930s, Coretta Scott would walk five miles each day on her way to a one-room school. She would watch as a school bus, which was filled with white children on their way to another school, would pass her. When she saw the bus, she wondered why black children and white children went to different schools and why white children were able to ride the bus while black children, like herself, walked. Even at this very young age, Coretta had a vision of equality for all people.

An intelligent and hardworking student, Coretta graduated at the top of her high school class, majored in music and education in college, and continued her music education at the New England Conservatory of Music in Boston. While at the conservatory, she accepted a lunch date with another student who shared her vision of equality. This date led to courtship by, and marriage to, Dr. Martin Luther King Jr.

With her husband, Coretta Scott King became an active leader in the civil rights movement. The words of Dr. Martin Luther King Jr., "I have a dream," have resonated throughout the world and will be quoted forever. Because of this dream, one which Coretta herself had envisioned since she was a small child, the couple made unprecedented progress in the movement toward equality and away from racial injustice.

When an assassin killed her husband, she continued the leadership of his work. Since then, she has created and overseen the Martin Luther King Jr. Center for Nonviolent Social Change in Atlanta, Georgia, and continues to speak out against injustice, especially racial injustice. Because of her efforts, her husband's birthday is recognized as a national holiday. Coretta Scott King is a visionary and a true leader, who has made a huge difference in the world.

Like Coretta Scott King, all leaders are visionaries. Father Theodore Hesburgh, former president of Notre Dame, said that vision "is the essence of leadership. [Knowing where you want to go] requires three things: having a clear vision, articulating it well, and getting your team enthusiastic about sharing it." In this section, Barbara Goodman ("Grand Opening Day, San Diego") shares her experiences and challenges in starting a new business. Because of her contagious enthusiasm, others shared in her vision and helped to make the business a success.

In *A Briefing for Leaders: Communication as the Ultimate Exercise of Power*, Robert L. Dilenschneider defines vision as "a clear course, which biases the organization toward action while giving people a sense of purpose above the everyday." Later in this section, Gayle Anne Kelley ("Visionary Thinking") elevates a schoolroom discussion about something as commonplace as bottled water into a look at the essentials for visionary leadership.

Linda Ahlers, president of Marshall Field's, was asked by a reporter whether she attained her position through a series of flukes or if this was something she aspired to achieve. Linda responded, "I knew pretty early on in my life what I wanted to do. Even before I went to college, I knew I wanted to be in retail. I had worked at my father's store doing bookwork and floor sales. I liked business. I liked financials. I liked interacting with people. Did I ever expect this—to be running Marshall Field's? Let me just say that I believe anything is possible."

In this section, you will see how Delores Ray ("Create Your Destiny") pursued her vision of becoming a stockbroker, even though at the time, "they did not allow women to be brokers" in her company. Like Linda Ahlers, she believed that she could achieve whatever she wanted in life.

The word "vision" derives from a word, which literally means "to see." A vision is an image, a picture of the future. In *The Leadership Challenge*, James M. Kouzes and Barry Z. Posner list four attributes of vision:
- Ideality—The pursuit of excellence

    Visions are ideals, or standards for excellence, and they begin with possibility thinking, not probability thinking.
- Uniqueness—Pride in being different

    Visions differentiate leaders in attracting and retaining followers, including employees, customers, and investors. This uniqueness fosters pride and boosts self-esteem of those associated with the vision.
- Future Orientation—Looking forward

    Leaders are proactive in thinking about and planning for the future. The more strategic the leader, the more future-oriented she is.
- Imagery—Pictures of the future

    Visions are image-oriented, rather than word-oriented. Leaders invent the future by first running a mental movie of what that future will look like.

All of the leaders who contributed to this book are visionaries. Through their vision, they have "seen" the future long beforehand, and they have acted on their vision. Most of them also engage in the practice of visualization on a regular basis. To me, visualization is intentional dreaming. It is taking the time to close one's eyes and picture the desired future.

When I first heard of visualization, I was skeptical. Already successful in business and considered a leader by many, I thought I didn't need to practice visualization. However, when I learned that Albert Einstein had said, "Imagination is more important than knowledge," I decided to give it a try. After all, I had considered Einstein to rank among the most intelligent people ever to live on this earth.

My first experiment with visualization was on a personal level, as I started visualizing selling my house and building my dream home. At the time, my house had been on the market for several months, and I had received no offers. I had bought a lot on a beautiful pond, and I needed to sell my existing home in order to start building. I visualized an immediate sale of my home to cash buyers who wanted to close and move in immediately. The following week, I received a cash offer! The buyers wanted to close in nine days and move in on the day of closing. As I put most of my belongings in storage and prepared to move into an apartment while my dream home was being built, I thought that the results of this visualization were almost spooky.

To confirm that visualization really worked, I immediately began to visualize other results in my life. My visualization included those things that many would have thought impossible, and my "creations" ranged from career advancement to material belongings to enhanced relationships to more spirituality. Within three months, all of my dreams/visions were fulfilled. I became a strong believer in the power of visualization.

Visualization is a technique that is used by world-class athletes, as well as by world-class leaders. These athletes experience their victories, over and over again, in their minds long before they experience them physically. Visualization is based on the principle that all things are created twice, first in the mind and then in reality. Athletes and visionary leaders understand exactly what Walt Disney meant when he said, "If you can dream it, you can do it."

Visualization is not new. Aristotle said that the soul cannot think without pictures. "The reasoning mind thinks in the form of images. . . . As the mind determines the objects it should pursue or avoid in terms of these images, even in the absence of sensation, it is stimulated to action when occupied with them."

The following process has created success for me, both in business and in life, and has significantly contributed to my effectiveness as a leader:

1. Determine what you want to create in your life or in your business.

   Without concerning yourself on the probability of achievement, start by making a list of your desired results. Since the subconscious mind works in present tense, make sure that your list is in present tense. Also, the items on your list must be expressed as the things you want, not the things you want to eliminate. Be positive!

2. Eliminate distractions.

   Go to a quiet place where you will not be distracted, close your eyes, and give yourself some time to unwind. If your mind wanders onto a trivial matter and you think you must remember it, open your eyes and write it down. Then close your eyes again and unwind.

3. Relax your body and your mind.

   If you have a favorite relaxation technique, use it at this point. One that I use is to tense and then relax muscle groups, one at a time, starting with my feet and working up to my forehead.

4. Create a mental movie.

   Eleanor Roosevelt said, "The future belongs to those who believe in the beauty of their dreams." As human beings, not only can we dream, but we can also make those dreams come true.

   Begin picturing your desired results as if they have already happened. The important word here is *picture*, as visualization works best in pictures, not in paragraphs. Dr. Dennis Deaton advises visualizing these pictures as sensory-rich, emotion-laden images. He says, "The more sensory-rich and emotion-laden the images, the more powerful they are to the subconscious, the more quickly they are absorbed, and the more readily they are acted upon."

   As you run your mental movie, envision yourself using all five senses—sight, hearing, smell, taste, and touch. Also, let yourself experience your feelings, both emotionally and spiritually.

5. Reinforce your vision through consistent mental rehearsal. Although visualization takes time from a leader's already busy day, it is time well invested. Through your thoughts, you are creating the future. Your mind will then drive your actions in the direction of your dominant thoughts.

Visualization is different from daydreaming. It is dreaming with a purpose, or intention. In *The Book on Mind Management*, Dr. Dennis Deaton states, "Vision is the element that integrates all of your faculties. When you visualize your goals in sensory-rich, emotion-laden images, you unite conscious mind, subconscious, and the energy and passions of the body into one unified force. The melding of all of your faculties vaults you to the highest attainable levels of human performance." He summarizes the process by the following four steps:

- The conscious mind activates the subconscious mind with the dominant thought.
- The subconscious mind develops plans to realize the dominant thought. It then flashes the plans to the conscious mind for evaluation.
- The conscious mind evaluates and approves the plans.
- The subconscious mind governs the body to bring the plans into working reality.

George Bernard Shaw said, "You see things, and you say, 'Why?' But I dream things and say, 'Why not?'" Like George Bernard Shaw, effective leaders engage in possibility thinking. They know that anything is possible, as is evidenced in the contributions of five female leaders in this section. In one of the following writings, "Lessons from Ancient Cultures," Andrea Epel Lieberstein relates how an experience on a mountaintop when she was seventeen later forged a vision that helped revolutionize wellness education at a major health maintenance organization.

Visions grow from ideas. In this section, Kimberly Anderson-Maggi (*Work for Your Dreams—Then Live Them*) tells of her idea of forming a security company, which grew into a multi-million-dollar business.

President Woodrow Wilson said, "We grow rich by dreams. All big men [and women] are dreamers. They see things in the soft haze of a spring day or in the red fire of a long winter's evening. Some of us let dreams die, but others nourish and protect them, nurse them through bad days till they bring them to the sunshine and light which always comes to those who sincerely hope their dreams will come true."

Like Coretta Scott King, you can be a visionary leader. Your dreams will come true, if you just dare to dream!

Grand Opening Day, San Diego

Barbara Goodman

Be willing to embrace possibility thinking. Sometimes a new possibility will show up small, like a porthole, barely catching our attention and seemingly insignificant, easy to overlook. As it beckons us to take a longer, closer look, that porthole can become a portal, growing into large, beautiful French doors. If you choose, you can catch hold of the latch, throw these doors wide open and sweep yourself through, entering an entirely new and fresh landscape you've never even dreamed existed.

Several years ago, Dan and I, friends from an earlier time period in our lives, reconnected in New York City, where I was living, for a casual, simple dinner. We fell in love and, within a short time, were planning our life together.

Six months later, after resigning from my corporate position and moving from Manhattan to Del Mar, California, I chose to immerse myself and focus on our mission, to build a life together and to build our dream and vision, a "California Attitude" company.

We were first-time entrepreneurs who had grown up in corporate America, Dan in retail merchandising chains, in senior vice president and general merchandise manager positions, and I in Fortune 100 companies in sales and project management. We were now setting sail on our maiden voyage on the seas of capitalism, the free enterprise system. Our flags were raised high, as were our hopes.

We purchased our first store from a T-shirt store owner who wanted out. Using money from "family and friends" and the bank, our prime location was in La Jolla, California. There was foot traffic in the evenings, the surfers hung out, locals dined, tourists frequented the spot, and everyone wanted T-shirts! As we worked in our new store in the early weeks and discovered what customers wanted, we discovered what the prior owner didn't know. He didn't know how to buy T-shirts that would *sell!*

What a surprise! We scurried around, securing more financing for new merchandise for the store. Then, in order to make better decisions on our new line of best-selling T-shirts, we took a crash course in the T-shirt business by researching every vendor. Grand opening day was coming quickly, and the register was eager to *ring*.

Soon the store was stocked full, brimming over with new circular racks with *the* hottest T-shirts of the day, guaranteed to attract our target market of locals and tourists and certain to get us known in town.

Our very expensive advertising splash to announce our grand opening was breaking for a Sunday in June. Dan's teenage daughters, Lisa and Lori Goodman, worked after school and weekends with us to help get the store ready and the new merchandise displayed. By Saturday night, Dan and I could take personal time together and have a real "date." Oh boy! After enjoying our date, as we were driving home, we decided to "just stop by the store for a minute" and look one more time.

We were like school-kids, so excited! We threw open the French doors, turned on all the lights and stood in the doorway beaming at our masterpiece. As we stared proudly and lovingly into the store, I noticed something . . . something black. "What is that black line running across the middle of the store?" I asked. "What black line?" he asked. I walked to the center of the store and discovered a thick parade of black ants about a half-inch wide trudging deliberately from the middle of the left wall across the carpet, up the closest T-rack, across the tops of all our new T-shirts, down the other side, across the carpet again, continuing all the way across the store, up and down all the racks of clothing and out past the door on the far right wall, as though marching to salvation! There must have been tens of thousands, moving in a continuous parade of exodus. "It's ANTS!" I gasped.

He immediately shouted in his passionate, excitable way, "Oh no, we're ruined! We're broke! It's opening day tomorrow, and we've got people coming into the store! We'll have to spray!"

Calmly, I reminded him that no one will buy a T-shirt that smells like bug spray! I sprouted a solution right where I was planted and announced, "Let's make it a *party!* Could you please find a rock station you love and turn on the music real loud? We'll open the doors and carry every T-shirt outside and shake and flick every ant off of each shirt. We'll work until it's done, get some sleep, and have our grand opening day tomorrow."

As we walked in and out through the French doors to the front sidewalk, each of us with the next T-shirt in our hands, lots of people came by asking about the store. Although we were not open for business that night, our great attitude, music and spirit attracted them. Many said they'd be back the next day. On Sunday, as we opened the store early and peered in, the ants had not returned. We were heartened and encouraged to see many familiar faces from the night before on our first grand opening day!

Why do I tell you this story? Why is it significant? What qualities of leadership are demonstrated here?

Although I had not wanted to stop by the store while on our "date," wanting us to value balance in our lives, Dan felt he had to, and decided to stop. I immediately dropped my personal agenda and supported him. That's teamwork. Once a decision is made, every member of the team fully supports the decision. A good leader is willing to follow. We simply take turns being the leader.

Dan had an innate sense of the importance of stopping at the store. He trusted in his own intuition and was not swayed from following it.

Once we were at the store and identified a problem, we changed leadership roles. In the problem phase, he was submerged in negative thinking, living in the problem. I shifted immediately to possibility thinking using my intuition and creative problem-solving skills, and I was patient with the certainty that a solution would be found. We turned a potential disaster into an enjoyable experience, solved a problem through teamwork, and attracted new customers beginning on Saturday night for our grand opening day. People buy us and our values first.

We were committed to our dream and mission. Our family life was woven around our business, and we lived our dream in the moment.

Good leaders recognize and encourage the strengths and values of each of their team members and use this knowledge to produce effective results. By Dan turning on the music, his energy switched immediately from negativity and fear to positive and enjoyable focused action.

Keeping the energy positive and high, glowing with enthusiasm, we created a celebration of all the hard work that culminated in a very successful grand opening.

Having a "no matter what" attitude, we cooperated with dedication and dependability, completing the task at hand, certain that we had covered all bases.

Making it fun at every possible juncture, laughing at circumstances and joyful at our results, we laughed and kidded around with the people who stopped by. "What ants?" we would ask.

Sunday, our grand opening day, was a great success! In the next few weeks, our new formula for a "California Attitude" company was working well, our location was proving successful, and Lisa and Lori were invaluable in their contributions to the company's growth. They provided ideas and worked as team members. They became examples of "French doors to possibility thinking."

The T-shirt business, though lucrative, begged for exposure in other merchandise areas. One day, Lori wore a pair of gorgeous

Vuarnet sunglasses home from school. Curious, baffled and intrigued, Dan asked her, "What are those?" and "Why did you buy them?" He held them in his hands, asking her how much she paid for them. She was reluctant to reveal the high price to him ($120–$150 in today's dollars). When she did, we had a huge "aha!" moment and immediately researched the sunglass marketplace. By adding sunglass lines to our marketing mix, these lines rapidly grew to be 50 percent of our business within the next two years.

We opened two more stores that first summer to test two additional business models. By September of the following year, we incorporated and opened our fifth store using the original model of "California Attitude" clothing and sunglasses, and using our newly incorporated name, Pacific Eyes and T's. Thanks to positive thinking, leadership, cooperation and openness to new ideas, we were well on our way to even greater success.

# # #

Barbara Goodman's joy is inspiring the human spirit, acknowledging one's many great qualities through authentic expression. She has consulted with entrepreneurs of start-up companies in positioning for attracting funding.

As a Certified Speaking Circles Facilitator in San Diego (www.speakingcircles.com) she helps people dissolve habits of self-consciousness and enjoy an increase in self-confidence, authenticity and magnetic effectiveness.

Barbara was co-founder and co-owner of San Diego-based Pacific Eyes and T's, a California Attitude clothing and sunglass store chain with $33 million in annual sales and thirty-six stores in four states. Her corporate experience was with Citicorp, NA, in New York City.

Visionary Thinking

Gayle Anne Kelley

I walked down the long corridor into the fifth-grade classroom. The children were waiting with eager anticipation for what I had to show them and for the stories I would share with them today. As a visiting lecturer on indigenous cultures, I am always excited to touch these young minds with sights and sounds and pieces of wisdom and art that have touched me. I, you see, have the glorious good fortune and, hence, responsibility to pass on what the native elders have so graciously taught me. There I was, once again, carefully placing my bag of treasures on a display table in front of the classroom of sixty smiling, shy, eleven-year-old faces full of anticipation.

Oh yes, and for reasons yet to be revealed, I also placed my sports bottle of Poland Spring water on that table. I always carry my water with me.

Thus it began—a magical, mystical, timeless walk. I gave them the greetings of the elders from many tribal nations, the Hopi, the Iroquois, the Lakota, etc. I showed them rattles and beautiful baskets made by hand. I told them stories about the wolf and the buffalo and the eagle. We talked about the winds and the sacred fire. I told them that these first peoples of the earth have made many wonderful contributions and have great secrets to share.

Then their eager questions came. They wanted to know more. In that moment, when I saw their passion, I picked up my bottle of water. Holding it in my right hand and lifting it high into the center of the room, I said, "Do you see this bottle of water? What does it mean that we are drinking bottled water?" As I looked around the room, I saw them gaze at several bottles of water sitting on their own desks.

"Who can tell me how much of the earth is water?" I asked. "And who can tell me what percentage of our body is water?" "Seventy-five percent of the earth," they shouted out, "and three-quarters of our bodies!" "My," I said, "water must be very important to our lives. Then, what is the message of the water in the bottle? What is it telling us?" A hush fell over the room. Their eyes were wide open, as they waited to hear what I would say next.

"You are correct," I said. "The earth is about 85 percent water, but did you know that only one percent of this water is drinkable, and we are polluting it? The old Indians would tell me that water is the first law of life, and we must protect it."

The children began to speak about not being able to swim at many of the beaches. They asked if this meant that the water wasn't healthy. Was their water safe to drink? We now have to buy water. Would prices go up in the future? They wanted to know how this happened. Didn't the people who were in charge see this coming? "Maybe they had no vision," I answered.

Visionary thinking is one of the most crucial skills that we must develop as a society. Advanced leadership understands that it must build, risk, inspire, and educate visionary thinking into the world.

When I think of visionaries, I think of those who hold a dream for a better world, a way to improve the human condition. A visionary is a person who truly sees and understands the interconnectedness of all things—thoughts and manifestation, the individual and the collective, the microcosm and the macrocosm, humankind and the natural world, yesterday, today, and tomorrow.

Visionary leadership starts with a partnership with higher reason, the realization that what we do affects others. Visionary thinking puts one into a more conscious relationship with cause and effect. Every action has a reaction, and we need to ask how our decision will affect everything around us. It begins to reinforce the idea of connectedness and community. Good leaders will help people to define their relationship to the bigger picture, thus creating a trans-formational environment where people really begin to understand that it matters not only what we do, but also how and why we do it.

I believe strongly that, in order for humanity to grow, we must develop a more balanced way of learning. This would include not only looking at how we can learn from the past but also asking for "eyes of understanding" that read the "signs" directly in front of us. Let us begin to pay attention and trust that we are constantly receiving information in the moment that will consciously help us to evolve. This new way of looking at change will lead us in more productive directions.

Good visionary thinking is guided by principles of healthy behavior that embrace one's values, beliefs, purposes, and goals. The vision must be inclusive and provide a common language spoken on common ground always empowering the future. Fostering visionary thinking requires that one seek a balanced life, clear thinking, courage, and a desire to serve the greater will.

Ultimate lasting success comes from the strength of your vision. It is a blueprint, a roadmap of where you are going. It forces you to raise questions about obstacles, impact, consequence, and possibility. The legacy of this type of leadership reflects upon ultimate power as being that which protects the rights of those unborn citizens yet to come.

I believe that, for women, true visionary leadership dwells within the architecture of our being. We are the life givers, as we give life to the future.

Dare to dream a future not yet realized but promised by an infinite universe with infinite possibilities.

# # #

Gayle Anne Kelley is an educational consultant, multicultural strategist, grassroots organizer, documentary filmmaker, and peace trainer.

She is founder and executive director of *A Circle of Women*, an organization that educates and inspires women to take leadership roles in developing a new generation of peacemakers.

Gayle has lectured and taught worldwide, made guest appearances on radio and television, and is writing her first book, *Developing the Peacemaker in the 21st Century: A Woman's Perspective*.

Create Your Destiny

Delores Ray

Having been in the business world since 1955, I have learned the importance of creating my own destiny. If you wait for others to promote you or for things to just happen, chances are you will be in the same place ten years from now. The keys to creating your destiny are:

1. Make your own opportunities.

Since this is a capitalist system, you will be able to get ahead. When I was a clerk typist, the woman at the next desk was making more money than I was, because she could take shorthand. Instead of resenting her, I went to school to learn shorthand.

2. Always do more than is required of you.

Too many people say, "That's not my job." By doing more than expected, people feel better about themselves and learn much more. This, in turn, makes the job more interesting. When I was a registered sales assistant at a major brokerage firm, they did not allow women to be brokers. However, I wanted to be a stockbroker, and I studied at night and on holidays. I then took the test and passed it. Even though I knew women were not allowed to be brokers, I thought by my doing more than was expected of me, someone would notice and give me a chance. That is exactly what happened. Do what is needed, prepare yourself ahead of time for opportunities, and the opportunities will come. Also, do something you enjoy doing. If you are absolutely in the wrong field, change fields—even if it is a slow process and even if it takes one small step at a time.

3. Have a positive attitude.

Don't hang around with complainers. Complaining can become a disease, not only of the mind but also of the spirit.

4. Decide what you want to do, and then do it.

If it takes more education, go to school at night or whenever you can. Small steps will take you a long way, and you will be surprised at how much you can accomplish. Getting started is the difficult part, so just start! You will also be surprised at who will provide opportunities for you when they see you are working toward a goal and growing. Those in management positions don't like to see stagnant people in their organizations, so work as if you owned the company.

5. If you are in a position to supervise others, encourage them to learn.

Don't be a boss who is intimidated by employees who report to you. Make their jobs interesting, and be sure to compliment them when they do well. Look at each person's skills, and bring out the best in each person. Too many supervisors try to get people to conform to their way of working. You will notice that creative people organize and work differently than analytical people. If you try to fit them into the wrong mold, this will not work, and they will become dysfunctional employees. Treat them with respect, and recognize that they can contribute much to the organization.

6. Visualize your goals each day.

Never give up. Visualization and persistence will help you to achieve your goals.

# # #

Delores (Dee) Ray is a senior vice president and investment executive with a regional investment company in Minneapolis, Minnesota. She was the first female senior vice president in her company and the first woman on its board of directors. She has been named one of twenty stockbrokers of the year by *Registered Representative* magazine, and her clients have been featured in *Money* magazine and *Ladies Home Journal*.

Work for Your Dreams—Then Live Them!

Kimberly Anderson-Maggi

My family has been in the security business for over seventy years, and I have grown up in this industry. I know almost everything there is to know about security; however, being a woman in the security field, plus owning and managing my own security business, is not an easy task.

Like many companies, mine started from an idea that I had in my head for years. When I brought the idea for my company to the attention of my family, they were very proud and wanted to help. My sister, Debbie Anderson, was the first to get on board with the idea, and we worked on the company for almost a year before we even brought home a paycheck. The two of us did every job that could be done, from bookkeeping to working as a security officer.

At first, I found it very difficult for me to stretch my time every day, taking care of the needs of both my company and my family. On a daily basis, much of my time is devoted to my five children, ranging in age from eight to twenty-one. I firmly believe that, above all that goes on in my life, my family always comes first; they, too, have always been supportive of me and of my ventures.

My company is now entering its sixth year. Our revenue has grown steadily from $1.102 million in the first year to $2.24 million in the second year to $2.626 million in the third year to $3.025

million in the fourth year to $4.28 million in the fifth year. Projected revenue for this year, after just contracting with our largest account, is $10 million. I feel very fortunate that my business has done so well; my company is currently listed as number eighteen in the security category in the *Arizona Business Journal*.

Since the inception of my business, I have found that dreams have become a powerful part of my success. Over time, they have been my inspiration as I have envisioned that the "impossible" is really possible. By living my dreams, I have been able to connect with other women like myself, and I have become encouraged through their dreams as well. I dream of wealth and happiness for my family and my friends. I also pass my dreams on to my children, so that they may have a better chance in the business world when they experience their own challenges. I believe the goals set around dreams enable us to significantly enhance our talents and abilities and look for opportunities and excellence in our own ways.

I encourage you to stay with your dreams until they come true, no matter how long it may take. Wouldn't it be wonderful if you could inject your dreams into your employees like a medication? How fast we could all reach the top of the mountain! How fast we could all wake up and discover fewer negative attitudes, less criticism, and more creativity!

Test your possibilities. Dreams are for everyone!

# # #

Kimberly Anderson-Maggi is founder and chief executive officer of Anderson Security Agency, Ltd. in Phoenix, Arizona. Her business grossed over $1 million during its first year and grew to be a multi-million-dollar business soon after that.

Lessons Learned from Ancient Cultures

Andrea Epel Lieberstein

I never thought much about being a leader. I simply followed my passion. When I am passionate about something, I follow my vision and manifest it in the world. This often looks like "leadership." My passions, which are based on deep spiritual values and convictions, led me to wonderful opportunities for greatly impacting the world of health care within a prominent health maintenance organization (HMO).

When I was seventeen years old, I was blessed with an experience on the top of a mountain in the Sierra Nevada that would form the direction of my work and my life and would clarify my passion and purpose. During the last day of a backpacking trip, while climbing alone to a high mountaintop, the world appeared to me in a whole new way. Surveying the gorgeous nature around me from this high perch, I felt completely at peace, connected with the radiant landscape, and at one with it at the same time. Feelings of indescribably delicious harmony flooded me, and a deep experience of knowing that this beauty and perfection of life was what was fundamentally true, overcame me.

I would never be the same again. My eyes, heart, and spirit had been opened to a way of being and seeing that I knew was an underlying reality accessible to all peoples. Taking my pen to paper—on pages that I still have today—I wrote that somehow my life would

25

be about bringing knowledge and experience of this underlying harmony, perfection, and peace to people. The medium and methods I would use for this were still unknown to me, but to be discovered.

There have been blessings, hard work, and moments of grace along this path. As I went through my studies in human biology at Stanford University, focusing on disease prevention, wellness, and healthy lifestyles, and later in graduate school at University of California at Berkeley, my deep internal conviction led and magnetized me to the circumstances, people, and jobs that would most help this vision actualize in the world. The discovery and practice of meditation and tai chi chih helped nurture my inner life.

Always remembering my vision, I chose to earn a master's degree in public health, because I loved the approach of impacting populations on a large scale rather than just one on one. Although I had many interesting consulting jobs after graduation, the one that would turn into an exciting career with the greatest possibility of affecting others' lives positively was at a Kaiser Permanente facility, an innovative healthcare organization in Northern California.

My first job at Kaiser proved to be an incredible outlet for my creativity and vision. I was interested in bringing what was still considered alternative modalities, such as meditation and yoga, to health education programs for outpatients at Kaiser. I was blessed with two bosses who shared my thinking. With the support of both of these people and a regional health education department that was also visionary, I wrote and received a grant, attended training, and piloted the first "Mindfulness Meditation-based Stress Reduction Program" at Kaiser in Northern California. This was based on the well-studied program developed by Jon Kabat-Zinn at the University of Massachusetts.

During my twelve years at Kaiser Permanente, I developed many curricula in the area of mind/body medicine and coordinated and taught a large behavioral health program. Bringing the mindfulness program on a large scale to the region was one of my greatest accomplishments and personal sources of satisfaction.

With the successful implementation of this program at one facility, I wrote further grants over two years. I also received funding to conduct three regional trainings to 150 health professionals, staff, and instructors in the Northern California Region to introduce the program regionwide and provide the necessary guidelines to implement it. The trainings were a success. The program is now part of the regional core class offerings and is offered in at least sixteen Kaiser facilities in Northern California. The number of lives that are affected positively by this continues to grow each year. Kaiser serves as a model for other medical centers as they begin to offer the program and can refer back to the widespread implementation at Kaiser. Because of this, I know that thousands of people are learning a new way of being, and they are finding ways to the peace and balance that I experienced on the mountaintop back when I was seventeen.

Overwhelmingly, I have been met with gratitude for pioneering these programs. Although, at times, I met resistance from those threatened by change of the status quo within the organization, I never worried much about the resistance. I just continued to follow my passion to bring these programs to the people. I found the right people in the organization who shared similar visions and worked on educating those who didn't. I learned that teamwork, shared resources, and cooperation are important elements for significant accomplishments and successful leadership. Pioneering efforts almost always meet with some resistance at first.

Meanwhile, in a path parallel to my professional life, I explored skillful ways to integrate spiritual reality into everyday physical reality through a series of local training workshops. Through movement, breath work, and exercises to expand limiting negative beliefs, I was led into new experiences and insights that were to further shape who I am as a woman and a leader.

I began to have experiences in my body, through movement and breath work that I'm sure many of our ancestors had as they danced around the fires or in their ancient rituals. I became aware of the tremendous power and strength in my body. This power radiated particularly from my pelvic and belly area, the area that in Chinese martial arts and in yoga is seen as the seat of power in the body.

No one had ever told me about this part of being a woman. I hadn't known that such feelings of power, connectedness, and even ecstasy could flood through me like this. My understanding of what it was to be a woman grew even larger than before, and it had never felt better. Although I was brought up by parents who told me I could accomplish anything and I had always felt good being a woman, these experiences brought home an internal knowledge of an even greater powerful potential and creativity that was naturally inherent in us as women. Yet, this has been obscured from us in contemporary culture, where so much of a woman's worth and self-esteem are tied up in maintaining external beauty and appearances, while other aspects of the feminine are devalued.

The media and advertising culture have created an oppression and preoccupation for most women where we focus on our appearances as our means to power and feelings of self-worth. As we age, a large amount of emotional and financial energy often goes into struggling against the natural occurrence of aging and changing appearances. There was a time when the original meaning of the word "hag" meant wise or holy woman. This is only one of many examples where things that were once positively associated with the esteem and power of women have taken on negative connotations in more recent times.

How much energy gets diverted from a woman's peace of mind and natural birthright of being a leader in her own unique way in her community, her family, her children's education, or her professional arena by being caught up in these kinds of struggles? I've learned that there is a very important hidden layer of innate strength and power, inherent beauty, and natural leadership that is so intrinsically connected to the earth's creative energy and to the cycles of the moon. It was acknowledged and celebrated in ancient rituals and celebrations, and we can feel this when we attune ourselves to the earth's natural cycles. This aspect of being a woman has remained hidden to us in mainstream culture.

In my desire to understand further, I turned to readings and new archaeological research on the history of women throughout time and the ancient goddess cultures. I discovered that there is a hidden history of women where we once were the leaders, the governors, the priestesses, the ritual mistresses, and the healers. The ancient rituals and practices, more than likely, facilitated these feelings of feminine power and leadership that I experienced on a regular basis. Women had an entirely different sense of themselves.

The ancient goddess cultures lived harmoniously for thousands of years and were peace-loving, artistic, egalitarian, and matristic until they were conquered, suppressed, and slowly swallowed or incorporated over centuries into the mainstream religions and cultures we know today. These ancient cultures promoted peace, cooperation, and ecologically balanced living. They were based around a belief in a great mother, a central creator goddess as their deity, and reverence for nature.

A new passion and purpose began to be born in me. I wanted to share this knowledge and these experiences with women to empower us to be the leaders, visionaries, and pioneers that is our birthright. I had accomplished my own pioneering work at Kaiser. By bringing programs on meditation and balanced living to an entire region, I was bringing the values of the ancient goddess cultures to health care before I even knew about them.

So many of us are already bringing those values to our lives and work. How empowering to know that we are not alone and that we have an ancient lineage that is calling to us and supporting us, even if we haven't been aware of it! By identifying our passions and sense of life purpose, we can naturally lead in the arenas of our lives that move us and that we love. Through getting in touch with the ancient role models and cultures that existed before our written history, sometimes hidden between the lines of our written history or in an ancient song or folktale, we can inform and inspire our present roles as female leaders and move forward into the future with a new vision of the possibilities of egalitarian, peace-loving societies. We have an important role to play in creating a new "Garden of Eden" on earth, where women can shine as the natural leaders we are.

# # #

For more than fourteen years, Andrea Epel Lieberstein, MPH, R.D. has specialized in helping people transform their lives through stress management, mindfulness training, nutrition, and lifestyle change. She was a pioneer in Kaiser Permanente, Northern California Region, creating stress management and mind/body curriculums, teaching classes, providing training of instructors, and implementing regionwide mind/body programs, such as Mindfulness-based Stress Reduction.

Andrea is writing a book with the working title, *Meeting the Power of the Goddess: Unveiling Our Hidden History*. She leads workshops for women on discovering the power of the goddess in their lives, and teaches and consults in stress management. She can be reached at andrea@stresslessnow.com.

Section II

Grow through Challenge!

Grow through Challenge!

Joan Eleanor Gustafson

Effective leaders challenge processes and the "status quo."

As a young couple was cooking their first big meal in their new home, the wife prepared a roast by cutting off the two ends before placing the roast in the oven. When her husband asked why she had cut off the ends of the roast, she replied that her mother had always done this. She then decided to phone her mother to learn the reason for doing this. When the mother's response was that *her* mother had done it this way, the couple phoned the grandmother. Grandma's reply was stated very simply when she said, "That was the only way the roast would fit into my roasting pan!"

How often in business, and in life, have you heard someone say, "But we have always done it this way"? In my studies of effective leaders, I've determined that all effective leaders challenge existing processes. They actually seek challenges and look for ways to innovate, to make things better. Leaders actually embrace change. Later in this section, Terry Swack gives an example of this in "Thriving on Change," where she describes how she transitioned her graphics design business into an Internet strategy and design firm.

Innovation, challenge, and change require the willingness to take risks. Citing several examples of what she calls "organizational bravery," Victoria Harker ("Leaders Are Risk-takers" in this section) discusses how each of us can become an effective risk-taker.

In *The Leadership Challenge*, James M. Kouzes and Barry Z. Posner say, "Whenever leaders experiment with innovative ways of doing things, they put themselves and others at risk. Yet if we want to lead efforts to improve the way things are, we must be willing to take risks; we must, to paraphrase Eleanor Roosevelt, do the things we think we cannot." Kouzes and Posner go on to give the following action steps for leaders to ensure that others derive the greatest benefit possible from change:

- Set up little experiments.
    Test a new idea or process by experimenting; however, remember that it's not necessary to wait until your product or process is perfect.

- Make it safe for others to experiment.
    Take whatever actions are required in order for people to feel safe and secure when testing a new idea.

- Eliminate firehosing (putting down new ideas).
    Since people like to cling to the familiar when confronted with change, they will often respond like firefighters hosing down a fire by dousing the ideas and extinguishing the enthusiasm. Leaders need to look for ways to eliminate firehosing and encourage innovation.

- Work even with ideas that sound strange initially.
    If an idea sounds strange and is rejected, there is a possibility of losing a potentially good idea. Also, the rejection causes people to hold back on offering new ideas.

- Honor your risk-takers.
    According to Kouzes and Posner, every organization should have an "innovators' hall of fame" filled with trophies, plaques, pictures, and other paraphernalia. They suggest rewarding good attempts, as well as successes.

- Debrief every failure as well as every success.
    Ask the following four questions:

What did we do well?

What did we do poorly?

What did we learn from this?

How can we do better next time?

- Model risk-taking.

    Encourage others to take risks by doing so yourself, and don't ask others to do that which you yourself would be unwilling to do.

- Encourage possibility thinking.

    Make sure that people can see the benefits.

- Maximize opportunities for choice.

    By giving people a choice of alternatives, you are more likely to be successful in obtaining their commitment.

- Make formal clothing and titles optional.

    Research studies show that informality creates better results during times of uncertainty.

In *On Becoming a Leader*, Warren Bennis states that leaders have curiosity and daring. Wanting to learn as much as they can, they are willing to take risks, to experiment, and to innovate. "They wring knowledge and wisdom from every mistake and learn from adversity."

At the age of eight, Norma Earl ("Never Give Up on Hope" later in this section) contracted polio. When the doctors told her parents that she would not walk again, they encouraged Norma to believe in her dreams. Norma not only believed, but she also worked hard to overcome this challenge. She recovered and went on to be a leader in business and in the American Business Women's Association.

Erica Jong said, "If you don't risk anything, you risk even more."

Change is inevitable in today's world. In his best seller, *Thriving on Chaos*, Tom Peters declares, "the world has not just turned upside down. It is turning every which way at an accelerating pace. . . . Today, loving change, tumult, even chaos is a prerequisite for survival, let alone success."

Anita Roddick, founder of The Body Shop, said, "Learn to love change. Feel comfortable with your own creative intuition. Make compassion, care, harmony, and trust the foundation stones of business. Fall in love with new ideas." Her business has grown from one small cosmetics shop in England to more than 600 stores worldwide.

Peter Drucker, the highly respected management guru, once proclaimed, "Whenever you see a successful business, someone made a courageous decision."

Paul G. Stoltz, Ph.D., author of the best-selling book, *Adversity Quotient: Turning Obstacles into Opportunities*, states, "Without adversity, we can never unleash our greatness." Many of the contributors to this section of the book attest to this in their writings. Rather than being consumed by a victim mentality, they looked at the major challenges in their lives as growth opportunities and say now that they have become strong leaders because of the adversities, rather than in spite of them.

Later in this section, you will read about Sara Arbel's ("Heroism and Leadership") discovery, as an adult, of her "humble and quiet" father's amazing life in Poland during World War II. Knowing of her father's heroism has helped Sara to become a leader.

When I interviewed Linda Chandler, who owns four companies, she stated, "True leaders have goals, dreams, and desires. They're unwilling to quit when the hurdles come up. It takes courage to lead, courage to be different, courage to believe enough in yourself and to sell your vision."

At an early age, Linda learned about the relationship of challenge, courage, and strength from her paternal grandmother. "From many points of view," she said, "my grandmother had a tremendous disadvantage in her life. She was both physically and economically challenged and was deaf most of her life."

As a young child, Linda wondered why her grandmother always wore long skirts and walked with a limp. When she finally asked why, she learned that, when her grandmother was a young mother with a seriously ill child, she carried this child for several miles through a major blizzard so that the child could receive medical treatment. Because of this, Linda's grandmother's leg had been frostbitten and later amputated. "My grandmother had a very difficult life," Linda remembered, "Yet she never complained. She was so strong."

Linda herself is a strong woman and an inspirational leader.

Helen Keller was another much-admired leader, who overcame major adversity in her life. Shut off from the world by an illness that left her blind and deaf at age eighteen months, Helen later grew into a highly sensitive woman who spent her life writing, speaking, and working for the betterment of others. Until the age of ten when Annie Sullivan came to be her teacher, Helen was uncontrollable. Through patience and care, Annie was able to teach Helen to speak and to live a "normal" life.

In 1904, Helen became the first deaf-blind person to graduate from college. While a student at Radcliffe, she began her writing career, which continued for fifty years. She wrote twelve books and numerous articles on blindness, deafness, social issues, and women's rights. She brought a message of love, courage, and hope to millions of disabled people. In his eulogy at her funeral, Senator Lister Hill said, "Her spirit will endure as long as [people] can read and stories can be told of the woman who showed the world there are no boundaries to courage and faith."

In the Helen Keller story, there is another great leader—Annie Sullivan, Helen's teacher, who is often called "the miracle worker." Some might say that Annie was just doing her job; however, by doing her job and by truly caring, Annie was able to bring a ten-year-old deaf-blind girl back into the world. Because of Annie's caring leadership, Helen was able to grow and make her enormous contribution to the world.

All of the women in this section of the book have faced challenges, and there are as many different challenges as there are individuals:

- The famous mail-order icon, Lillian Vernon ("Leading during Difficult Times"), faced a critical financial challenge when her customers' needs were growing more quickly than her company's infrastructure.
- Lois Joy Crandell Hofmann ("Nature's Lessons on Leadership") learned to "let go" when violent weather threatened her personal dream of sailing around the world.
- Wendy Franz Richards ("Unaccustomed Challenges") and her fellow citizens mobilized to uphold the democratic process, producing positive results for their community.
- Marion Lonn ("Dare to Wear Your Red Shoes") dealt successfully with a multitude of life transitions, including culture changes, as her company transferred her young family around the world.
- Karen Carter ("Survivor Skills Lead to Achievement") discovered that many women leaders had overcome devastating setbacks in their lives and had become successful leaders as a result, as Karen herself had.
- Robin Muscia ("You DO Have a Choice") faced a most harrowing challenge at the hand of an abusive husband. Leaving all her worldly possessions behind, she moved across the country to start a new life and is now a leader both in business and her community.

Strong leaders grow through challenges. They challenge processes and the "status quo," look for ways to innovate, and embrace change. They establish a sense of urgency, create short-term wins, and are excited about the future. By doing so, they are creating opportunities for growth. In "Passionate Leadership" later in this section, Maggie Rogers talks about her enthusiasm for life, which translates into a gift for leadership. She is an inspiring example of someone who is always growing and bringing others along with her.

French philosopher Henri Bergson once said, "To exist is to change, to change is to mature, and to mature is to go on creating oneself endlessly."

May you go on creating yourself endlessly!

Leaders Are Risk-Takers

Victoria Harker

Leaders are risk-takers, but they take rational, reasoned, well-analyzed risks. They lead organizations to excellence through their own aggressive pursuit of challenging goals that may seem impossible to the uninitiated. Leaders intuitively know when critical risks are needed, and they willingly step into the breach, knowing that sometimes they will be successful and hit a home run, but sometimes they will fail.

To be an effective risk-taker, leaders must:

- Get comfortable making decisions quickly and with less than perfect information.
- Develop a thick skin to combat criticism, deal with errors, and make mid-course corrections without taking them personally.
- Hone their own analytical abilities to facilitate situational assessments that cut to the core of a decision.
- Take responsibility for the inherent risks in being the one making a decision.

Call it "organizational bravery". . . a professional Purple Heart.

But exactly how do true leaders do all of this?

They do it by being bold and willing to operate outside of their own personal comfort zone, each and every day.

The need for these kinds of leaders emerges constantly, all across the corporate landscape. Corporations need leaders who are willing to wade into battles large and small, while handling family responsibilities and dealing with Wall Street's expectations. Leaders do this while also balancing their employees' motivational needs.

True leaders have the psychological mettle to accomplish this balancing act of work and home. The good news is that, over the past decade, we have begun to breed a special kind of female leader who is willing to get into the bunkers and fight for and with her people to achieve truly great things.

More so than at anytime in history, the marketplace in the United States—whether it's the marketplace of commerce, or public service—has begun to reward female leaders who are serious about risk-taking.

Think of Meg Whitman at eBay, heading up the world's first on-line auction house, who claims she is no technical whiz. She leads by example, risking the company's future direction based on what her customers tell her they want and how and when they want it. She is brave enough to make difficult decisions, even when they might seem to fly in the face of conventional wisdom. That is precisely why eBay is trading at a much higher multiple today than Amazon, in essentially the same space.

Think of Madeleine Albright, the highest-ranking woman to serve the U. S. government, as the first female secretary of state, in the Clinton administration. She recently told an audience of executive women that even at age fifty-six, while attending her first NATO meeting, she suffered from the same self-doubts and insecurities as many women. As a result, she spent her first half hour in that meeting assessing the political landscape for "vibes" and internally crafting her message . . . until she realized that thirty-five minutes had passed and she had said nothing. And more significantly, the United States had said nothing on important human rights issues.

Once she realized this, she quickly gathered her thoughts and made a few bold but well-positioned statements, drawing upon her in-depth knowledge gleaned as an academic in Soviet affairs. She had taken a risk, to be sure, but a well-thought out, rational one to best serve the fate of many. Most importantly, many nations then followed the lead of the United States in that specific set of human rights policy-making.

Consider Lieutenant Colonel Rhonda Cornum, U. S. Army flight surgeon, who was held captive for eight days during the Gulf War. When questioned on her motivation for leaving friends, family, and a secure position as chief surgeon on a domestic Army base, she said, "The qualities that are most important in all military jobs— things like integrity, moral courage, and determination—have nothing to do with gender. Everyone volunteers to serve in their own way . . . no one in this country is coerced. We are paid for two things in the Army . . . the jobs we do daily and our willingness to risk our lives if called to war. This means, with equal opportunity we have equal responsibility to do our very best, leading with bravery and honor." She is a born leader and a risk-taker, to be sure.

As chief financial officer of a $15 billion company, the greatest leadership challenge I face is being a fiscally sound risk-taker in the heart of the tumultuous telecommunications industry. With the speed of regulatory and technological change, leadership requires reasoned risk taking to make the decisions that will have long-lasting effects on my company's financial performance. It is exhausting, exhilarating, frustrating, and freeing. Effective leadership demands that leaders not be faint of heart.

MCI is a company born out of regulatory change—the dismantling of the Bell system in 1984—and it has not slowed its rate of change since then. The Telecommunications Act of 1996 is a great example of a new set of regulatory requirements that mandated that we engage in smart risk-taking to implement in a cost-effective way, while serving the needs of our customers. By mandating the financial and systemic requirements for entry into both local and long distance for all telecommunications new comers, the Act required that we change the way we approach our existing long distance franchise, while branching out into local service as a new way of providing end-to-end communications service.

The financial impact and operational decisions inherent in making these strategic changes requires reasoned risk-taking. In order to do this, I must quickly and extensively access volumes of data through sequential iterations, culminating ultimately in intuitive leaps at the end of the process, trying to predict future performance that will maximize both revenue and profits. Frequently, millions of dollars will depend on these intuitive leaps, and they are not for the timid!

On their face, decisions like these can be overwhelming for many people, both men and women, because the technology and communications fields can be complex and unfamiliar. Also, these fields change so quickly, erasing a permanent baseline. Despite my own experience and the demographics of MCI, I often hear that these perceptions cause other women to avoid career opportunities in a truly exciting field. On a purely selfish level, they deprive businesses like mine of the critical talent we need to keep growing at our strong rate.

Right now, I am concerned about these fears of risk more than anything else in the industry, which is so very reliant on creative, intelligent human capital.

It's so important for everyone to know that women (and men) have vast opportunities in the high tech field today, if they can find it within themselves to be brave decision-makers and leaders. Others will follow. The corporate guerrillas, who were more interested in challenging the establishment than in working for it, defined MCI's corporate personality. They were natural born risk-takers. They risked their careers, and reputations, to build a brave new business, without an established network to assist them in building a strong business.

These corporate guerrillas had to judge talent that comes in nontraditional packages in an environment where the whole company, quite literally, could prosper or crash on the decisions of a handful of individuals. People who took those risks created a new corporate culture and were richly rewarded by the explosive growth of a brand new sector . . . a culture of leaders and risk-takers that still defines MCI today.

How do you become a risk-taker?

For me, it is a continually evolving process of discovering, tackling, and then mastering new challenges, both personally and professionally. By allowing yourself to constantly be at the bottom of the learning curve, you force yourself to risk failure and make demands of your ability to make decisions on the fly. I have personally done this by developing interests in new areas (like systems and operations), requiring me to learn basic functionality while making complex decisions day-to-day. Learning to compete as a triathlete, when I had previously not swum or biked competitively, also helped. So did learning to be a successful wife and mom to three little boys—which I am still working at every day!

In leading through risk-taking, you will encourage others to be of brave heart and do the same. They will follow you to learn the way.

Risk-takers lead because they know this and are acutely aware that life doesn't always give you a second half to play. So get out there and lead the charge . . . today!

# # #

Victoria Harker is chief financial officer and senior vice president of operations and information technology at MCI, a $15 billion publicly traded company. She manages information technology and operations, as well as all financial planning, business development, and analysis functions. Her educational background includes a bachelor of arts degree in English and economics from the University of Virginia, and an MBA from American University.

Unaccustomed Challenges

Wendy Franz Richards

Life pulls things out of you. So, if you want to find out what's in you, expose yourself to unaccustomed challenges.—John Gardner

Little did I know that I would fight so hard to uphold the democratic process—democracy, as I believe it was designed to be. The catalyst, which pulled me into action, was the appearance of "story poles" for a proposed construction project that spanned across our favorite local street. The size and scale of the building threatened to totally overshadow our town, our pocketbooks, and our sense of community. As a leader in business, with a successful career in telecommunications finance, this was my first foray into the public arena. Like everyone on our team, I was called to action, applying my business experience and management expertise for the betterment of our town.

Building a grassroots community alliance to challenge the will of city hall presented an unexpected and unaccustomed challenge. What made the challenge especially delicate was the fact that the project was a planned public safety building, providing new facilities for the local fire and police services. While there was, and continues to be, complete agreement in town that upgraded facilities are needed, a building as grandiose as the proposed design, situated square across our local main street and extending nearly the length of a football field, would have been out of place in our quaint, artistic community. The surrounding structures date back before the turn of the last century and are filled with small businesses, shops, and restaurants serving the local community. In short, the plan was too big and too expensive, phrases which later adorned campaign posters on houses throughout the town.

Despite significant citizen opposition, the project was pushed ahead, approved by city planners and city council alike. I watched as the concerns I raised in public forums, concerns which were voiced by hundreds of like-minded fellow citizens, were apparently belittled and ignored by our town officials. This brought forth an unexpected sense of injustice, of democracy being trodden upon in the name of "leave it to the experts, because we know what is best for you and your town."

A group of concerned citizens filed an appeal against the project, and the city council opened hearings. In the midst of this process, the tragedy of September 11, 2001, struck, changing forever our sense of safety and security and bringing into the forefront the bravery and dedication of our public safety personnel. I asked myself, as did so many people, "Should this horrible event cause us to reevaluate our priorities and 'give in' to the massive new plan? Is there not a way to provide adequate facilities and, at the same time, maintain a balance in our financial resources and the ambiance of our town?" Thanks to the outspoken leadership of a small group of citizens, regular meetings began to be held at a small café to determine how to galvanize public opinion to achieve a balanced solution. I, too, was moved to action.

Initially, our job was fact-finding, to understand how this decision had come about and what elements could be re-used for a more acceptable plan. We established an "audit team" to review all the city documents relating to the plan, applying our business and management skills to this issue. It soon became apparent that much of the work in designing the new facility had been done without broad-based public input and without a study of the impact on businesses and traffic patterns. Furthermore, a decision had been made early in the planning stages to combine what had previously been separate fire and police facilities, thus predetermining the need for one oversized building rather than two smaller ones.

People in town became hungry for information. At one city council meeting, I was one of four citizens providing information that we had compiled in our "audit." When the council sought to limit the time we had to speak, members of the audience cried, "Let them speak! We want to know!" I made it my job to demystify the financing plan for this project. Others on our team brought their expertise to bear in arenas such as architecture, real estate project management, program analysis, and marketing communications. Our mission was to discover and present the facts.

Eventually, the council agreed to put it to the people for a vote, in exchange for the removal of the appeal and litigation, launching the town into an election campaign. This was our first key victory, a huge success, and the culmination of several months of citizen action. This was the essential step that opened the door to real involvement in the town. We had the opportunity to bring this issue fully into the public eye, launching our campaign by sending a citywide mailing with specific information on the proposed building and possible alternatives. This began a public education campaign where our goal was to present the facts, build broad-based support, and move people to action by casting their vote in favor of alternatives.

Being a member of the senior team that led the campaign ranks among the most unique leadership experiences of my entire career. We were truly a team of leaders, mostly new to the arena of local government, who came together like an all-stars sports team ready to tackle a new and unique challenge. For the leader of our team, the role was that of shepherd, keeping the flock together, moving "this herd of cats" forward in unison. As the needs of the campaign evolved, individuals with relevant expertise stood up to take responsibility for various tasks, volunteering their energies where they saw the greatest opportunity to make a difference. One of our local business owners said, "When I thought about the people who will live in our town in the years ahead, I did not want them to say I let this thing happen. Not on my watch."

In the campaign, I continued to illuminate my fellow voters regarding the true impact on our town's financial resources and the need for future taxes to pay for the structure. When supporters of the plan told voters about a possible $2 million federal grant, for example, I picked up the phone and called Washington to get the facts about this particular source of funds. Speaking with the relevant House subcommittee, I learned that the average grant last year was only $220,000 for our state, a far cry from the promised $2 million.

Those in favor of the facility positioned it as a safety issue, rather than the building design issue that it was. Many residents I met opposed the project, yet declined having a sign on their property, out of fear that the fire or police services would somehow give them less service in time of need—an unfounded but nonetheless common fear. This fear was evidence of the depth of controversy created for the town, pitting neighbors against neighbors, which took quite a toll on us all.

What were the lessons for leadership? We focused on the facts, providing the voters with the real information they desired, challenging the status quo with solid data. Like any marketing effort, it was necessary to appeal to different "niche markets" among the populace. There were those who did not want to close the street, those who felt the building was simply too big, others whose primary concern focused on taxes and the cost of the building, voters who were concerned about an imposing structure creating the feeling of a "police state," those who distrusted the process that had resulted in this design, and those who felt other alternatives, which had been overlooked, would better represent our town. It was our job to provide the information needed to make an informed decision, mobilize all the various points of view, and bring people to the polls on election day.

With the efforts of a small core group of a dozen people, we learned many lessons as we progressed, seeking ways to enhance our productivity in reaching as many voters as possible. Like any business venture, we sought new "distribution channels," encouraging our supporters in turn to speak with their friends and neighbors. As a grassroots movement, we solicited small donations, which gave our supporters a concrete way to express their loyalty to the cause. In the end, we resembled a multi-level marketing organization, in that many friends and neighbors were involved, each in their own way.

On election night, as the returns came in, it became clear that our efforts reflected "the will of the people." We won a landslide victory—two to one—with 66.37 percent of the vote. In addition, in an election in which less than one-third of the state voters turned out, we had, reportedly, the largest ever voter turnout for a primary election, nearly 55 percent in our town. It was clearly a victory for the democratic process. We had challenged the status quo, and won. Along the way, we opened up the town for debate and discussion and developed incredibly close friendships in a group of successful, respected professionals from a variety of fields. This is an excellent demonstration of how business experience and management training apply directly to improving the community in which we live.

The challenge now for our elected leaders is to bring together all the citizens of the town and design a solution that can be agreed upon by the majority. As citizens and voters, we all have the opportunity and the responsibility to continue the active, participatory democracy, which we rekindled in our town.

# # #

Honored by CNN/*Fortune* magazine as one of "Europe's Most Powerful Women in Business," Wendy Franz Richards is a leader in finance and business development in the international telecommunications and media sector. She is founder and president of MarTel Advisors, Inc., providing strategic and financial consulting services and interim executive management for early stage ventures, serving investors in financial services, professionals, and management teams in telecommunications, media, and technology.

Wendy Richards served as chief financial officer and executive vice president corporate development for Europe Online. In Europe, she also held executive leadership positions at HSBC Investment Bank, Plc. and AirTouch Communications (now Vodafone), where she served more than a decade in building the world's leading provider of wireless communications

She holds an MBA from the Stanford Business School and speaks German, French and Greek. She can be contacted at www.marteladvisors.com.

Leading during Difficult Times

Lillian Vernon

A half-century ago, when I was a pregnant housewife with a desire to supplement my husband's income, I founded Lillian Vernon Corporation at my kitchen table. Since then, I have been through my share of stock market slumps, recessions, and wars, including the horrific tragedy on September 11, 2001.

Before World War II, if it had not been for my father's wisdom, our family would have perished. Luckily, we managed to escape the Nazis by moving to Holland, and then to the United States, where we settled in New York City. Experience has taught me that surviving difficult times is a matter of exercising decisive, careful judgment and strong leadership.

When the economy slows, companies with strong leadership can continue to grow. First and foremost, a leader must project optimism and be a positive role model for the rest of the company to follow. Negativity lowers morale, causing productivity to fall and valuable people to leave. Because I believe that a positive spirit always prevails, I feel it's essential to project optimism by showing my staff that teamwork and dedication pay off. My managers and I have a vision for our future and a plan for attracting new business and growing our company. Everyone at our company is included in our plan and made to feel a part of our team in order to achieve our goals.

Much of our fifty-one-year success can be attributed to the valuable input we receive from our staff. It has been my ongoing practice to conduct regular company-wide meetings to ensure that everyone works together in generating new ideas. My open-door policy has worked well. I meet weekly with my management team, and I work daily with my merchants, who travel overseas with me several times a year to select new products for our catalogs and Web sites. Our company has an employee suggestion program, rewarding employees for recommending innovative ways to increase sales and save money. Besides our customer focus groups, our next best source of information is input from the employees, as many of them fit the profile of our average customer.

A successful leader will go the extra mile and have the courage to take risks. This was the case in the 1980s, when, with the increasing popularity of 800 numbers and credit cards, our company was growing too fast, and we didn't have the infrastructure or the technology to keep up. I found myself needing to quickly expand our operations and increase our payroll to meet the growing needs of our business. To make matters worse, our fulfillment was slowing because our computer systems couldn't keep up with the orders. Updating our technology would cost millions of dollars, money we didn't have. My only escape from the threat of bankruptcy was an immediate infusion of cash, which a bank loan could provide. I decided that it was worth incurring debt to save the company so I acquired a $13 million bank loan. The loan was a risk, but it paid off in time for our busiest holiday season. We were able to pay our bills and install new, more sophisticated computer technology, dramatically improving our fulfillment operations and meeting the needs of our customers.

In the retail industry, a smart leader knows that the key to customer loyalty is providing the best customer service possible. At Lillian Vernon, we know from experience that treating our customers with care and making them feel special keeps them loyal. We often reward our best customers with free gifts and free shipping.

We guarantee 100 percent satisfaction on all our merchandise, including those items that are personalized. If a customer wants to return an item, we'll issue a replacement or refund, even ten years after an item was purchased. I welcome customer letters and e-mails, which I read faithfully so I don't lose touch with their needs.

Ultimately, the greatest risk for a leader is indecisiveness. If you're unwilling to make tough decisions and take risks, you will fail. Like President Harry Truman proved when he ended World War II with one critical, yet difficult decision, those who make hard choices must do so to survive.

# # #

More than five decades ago, Lillian Vernon founded Lillian Vernon Corporation, which she still leads. Her company, a national catalog and on-line retailer, publishes eight catalog titles and ships more than 5.6 million packages per year. With annual revenue in excess of $259 million, Lillian Vernon Corporation employs over 5,300 employees at the height of the Christmas season.

A lifelong philanthropist, Lillian has donated funds and merchandise to over 5,000 nonprofit organizations. An inductee into the Direct Marketing Association Hall of Fame, she is a role model and inspiration to millions of American women.

Lillian Vernon's on-line catalogs are at www.lillianvernon.com and www.ruedefrance.com.

Never Give Up on Hope

Norma Earl

I was just eight years old when *it* struck. After I'd been in bed with the flu for several days, Mother finally agreed that I was well enough to come downstairs and eat ice cream with my sister and brother. That's when *it* happened—my eyes rolled up into my head; I stiffened, still clutching the ice cream spoon in my hand.

I couldn't move; I was paralyzed from the neck down. I had polio.

After three months in an Omaha, Nebraska, hospital, I was sent home with the devastating news that I would never walk or talk again.

My father refused to accept that prognosis. Every day, seven days a week for three years, my father took me to the various therapy sessions—speech therapy, exercise therapy, steam treatments. Oh, how I fought him. I was miserable every minute of those three years.

Still, my father would not give up. He told me, "Take one day at a time, Norma; one goal at a time." He promised me that if I worked hard and got better, he would send me to modeling school, my childhood dream.

Together we worked for three years to rebuild my strength and agility. My father never gave up hope. Within a year, I was able to speak again. Within three years, I was back to "normal." I had missed two-and-a-half years of school, and had to put my nose to the grindstone to catch up with my classmates. But I was able to graduate from high school on time. And I got my wish—I enrolled in modeling school.

These early years shaped and influenced my life, giving me the tenacity and the strength to meet life's continuous challenges with optimism and focus. I learned an important lesson from my father: Never give up on hope.

After modeling school, I went to work at Mutual of Omaha, but the company didn't meet my expectations. I needed to grow; I needed more challenge. So I left to work as a bookkeeper at a night-club, learning all I could and working my way up to manager. Eventually, I bought my own steakhouse.

I was very successful in the restaurant business. Using the same hard work and tenacity I learned during the therapy years, I brought a mediocre dining establishment to high-profile profitability. I focused on treating customers as I wanted to be treated and made sure that the food would make them want to come back. It wasn't easy; I accomplished all this while married with two children.

And then came the challenge that would test all that I knew about life and motherhood—my husband's six boys came to live with us.

I sold the restaurant and joined my husband in the development of a data processing company. I was able to stay home while serving as office manager. We built a good business, George and I, but every day, the children presented a new challenge. Eight children, a husband, a business . . . I needed a break!

That's when I joined American Business Women's Association (ABWA) with the original intention of getting out of the house one night a month. When I saw the women being recognized for leadership at the annual ABWA national convention that first year, I decided then and there to become a leader, too. Here was a new challenge, and I dove in head first.

Since then, I have devoted my energies to ABWA. I have worked at chapter level in both Nebraska and Arizona, sharing the leadership opportunities with other working women like myself. I have held chapter and district office; spearheaded community service projects; and chaired committees for workshops, luncheons, and the national convention. I see ABWA in the same way I saw my father—always there, always supportive, always believing in me.

My husband and I went on to found Mr. Clutch USA, a licensing business of automotive repair shops. For many years, I was on the road twenty-five weeks out of fifty-two, building relationships and growing the business. Wherever I went throughout the country, ABWA was there for me. Building on the lessons learned in my early years of rehabilitation, I developed the focus, the vision, and the confidence to achieve all my professional and personal goals— taking one day at a time.

So when hope is elusive, when your trials are too much and the road seems all uphill, never give up on hope.

# # #

Norma Earl is the secretary/treasurer and director of dealer relations for Franchise Acquisition Corporation. Her twenty years of experience with the company and its predecessors include over ten years as a field supervisor for Mr. Clutch USA, overseeing as many as eleven auto-repair shops and opening new facilities. *Inc.* magazine nominated Norma and her husband for their "Entrepreneur of the Year" award.

An active member of the 80,000-member American Business Women's Association for thirty years, Norma has been honored locally by the association as "Woman of the Year" and a "Top Ten Nominee." On the national level, she served as a District VI vice president. Currently, Norma serves the ABWA as an ambassador.

The Effects of Stress on Leadership Ability

Bobbie Stevens, Ph.D.

Let's look at some of the qualifications necessary to be a good leader.

1. Lots of energy
2. Clear perception
3. A creative mind/curiosity
4. A strong desire to make a difference/contribution
5. Ability to remain calm in the midst of chaos
6. Ability to visualize and create a clear vision
7. A high tolerance for ambiguity
8. Willingness to take risks
9. Willingness to take full responsibility for results
10. Ability to stay focused
11. Ability to make and keep commitments
12. Well-developed intuitive abilities

These are a few of the abilities essential for good leadership. How do we get and maintain these abilities? Are we natural born leaders?

Many children have a number of these characteristics. Yet through the process of growing up, these abilities are diminished. Why?

The answer is **"stress."** As a society, we have overlooked the relationship between health and abilities, and how stress affects both.

Every time we have more stress in our lives than our nervous systems can handle, our health and abilities are affected.

Dr. Hans Selye, who dedicated his life to the study of stress, defines stress as any demand made on the body. According to this definition, all stress is not bad. It plays an important role in our lives. However, when more demands are made on the mind/body system than it can adequately handle, the entire system is damaged. Each time this occurs, our energy is decreased, and our nervous system becomes a little less capable of providing clear perception. As our energy decreases, we have less and less desire to make our contribution, and we become less and less capable of doing so.

As leaders, we make many demands on ourselves on a daily basis. In addition to all the demands of our business in the highly stressed environment where we usually find ourselves, we have all the demands of taking care of our homes and families. All of these demands are many times more than the ordinary nervous system can handle. Therefore, something has to give. All of the essential abilities necessary to be a good leader are diminished.

If we want to stay healthy and increase and strengthen our leadership abilities, we need to create a lifestyle that releases stress and strengthens our nervous systems on a daily basis. Our lifestyle is a reflection of what we think we need to be doing to fulfill our needs and desires. However, most of us have overlooked the importance of taking care of ourselves. When we deplete ourselves while serving others, in the long run, we are taking from everyone in our lives.

Many years ago when I was in college studying business management, I began to wonder what makes it possible for some people to be enormously successful while others fail. I knew it had to do with our thinking and behavior, so I decided to study psychology. Eventually, I discovered the works of Abraham Maslow. While Maslow was in college, he observed that some people functioned on a completely different level than the average person. He studied these people and coined the term "self-actualized" to describe them.

He discovered that they were the healthiest, and also the happiest, people in our society. They were highly creative, highly intuitive, and highly accomplished.

I knew that if some people could function from this more advanced level, then it had to be human potential. There had to be some way of developing this more advanced way of functioning.

Many years later, I discovered a process for the development of self-actualization. This discovery was quite by accident on my part. I was looking for a way to quit smoking when I found an article in a magazine about some breathing exercises that would help one quit smoking. I contacted the teacher and learned the breathing exercises. She also taught me some stretching exercises. I then found a book on meditation and focusing techniques. With all of my new discoveries, I developed a process that I started doing on a daily basis, and my whole life changed. I quit smoking, and many other things also happened: my energy started increasing, and I began to feel younger and more confident. My mind became very clear, and then I discovered that I knew things that I had no way of knowing. I became very calm and peaceful; I found that I could become quiet and ask questions, and I would get answers. One of the questions I asked was, "What role do we each play in creating whatever we experience in our lives?" I got a complete unfolding within my mind about how this process works. I could see that there are laws of nature, or principles of life, that determine how we all create whatever we experience. I knew how it works, and I knew that I could create whatever I wanted to create for myself. I could see that there is a process that we can use to create whatever we choose.

I realized that I was experiencing what Maslow had described as experiences of self-actualized people. It was like moving into a whole new world. I had never experienced being so in charge of my life. I knew why things happen as they do and how I could work with these principles to create my life the way I wanted it to be.

I started a new company to see how my discovery would work in business. It worked exactly as I knew it would. I made lots of money, had lots of fun, and fulfilled my vision. I accomplished things that I would never have been able to accomplish before. However, I did run into one problem. Because I didn't really know what I was doing at the time, I stopped working with my breathing exercises, stretching exercises, meditation, and focusing techniques. Gradually my energy started decreasing, my mind wasn't quite as clear, and it was becoming just a little more difficult to accomplish the things that I had been accomplishing with ease. I then knew that I was moving back to my ordinary way of functioning. I didn't want this to happen, so I took some time off to discover what had happened for me and why. What I came to understand is that the process of breathing exercises, stretching exercises, meditation, and focusing that I was doing on a daily basis had released the stress that had accumulated in my nervous system. In other words, they had revitalized my nervous system and allowed me to move to this more advanced way of functioning. I knew that my purpose in life was to understand this and share it with others.

After experimenting with what I had learned and creating a few more things for myself, one of which was an ideal mate with whom to share my life, I put together a program to help others discover how to move to this new way of functioning and how they can create the life they want for themselves.

My husband and I have now been providing these programs for more than twenty years. We have had thousands of people participate in them with outstanding results. I also designed an executive development program, which we have provided for many Fortune 500 companies as well as many smaller ones.

I am well aware of the connection between health and leadership abilities. People tell me that they do not have time to do the process that I recommend on a daily basis. My answer is, "It is not about time. We all have the same amount of time. It is about choice." I guarantee you, if you make a choice to take care of yourself first, you will have more free time. What we discover is that, when we function better, we can do less and accomplish more in the same time frame.

It is possible to create a lifestyle where we take care of ourselves on a daily basis and increase, within ourselves, all twelve of the leadership qualifications previously listed. It is possible to take charge of our lives and create them the way we want them to be. It is simply a matter of choice.

# # #

Dr. Bobbie Stevens holds doctorates in both psychology and business management. She is the author of *Unlimited Futures: How to Understand the Life You Have and Create the Life You Want.* She is president of Unlimited Futures, LLC. For more information, visit her Web site at www.UnlimitedFutures.org, contact Tara Publishing via e-mail at TaraPublishing@att.net, or call toll free (866) 563-1493.

Nature's Lessons on Leadership

Lois Joy Crandell Hofmann

After successfully growing a biotechnology company from ten to one hundred employees, taking it public, and serving as its CEO for four additional years until I retired, I began a new journey. My husband and I ordered a forty-three-foot, semi-custom, oceangoing catamaran with the goal of sailing it around the world.

We began Voyage One of our circumnavigation by sailing our new cat, called *Pacific Bliss*, from the shipyard in the south of France to our home in San Diego, almost 10,000 miles. We are now one-third of the way toward our goal, and we plan to sail to the Marquesas, in the South Pacific, the first leg of Voyage Two, this spring.

When I first talked with the author of this book about how getting our boat from one port to another involves leadership, the obvious connections came to mind. They included management of the crew we had on board for long passages—such as crossing the Atlantic—and their interaction in the confined space of the boat, provisioning, the challenge of encountering strange situations and different languages and cultures, and dealing with fear and boredom.

I realized that relating *this* experience—circumnavigating the world—to the skills I needed to lead a company was only the tip of the iceberg. It went much deeper than that. There were so many lessons that Nature taught me that can apply to the rest of my life.

The biggest lesson was this: *You are not in control.*

After September 11, 2001, one of the most difficult things we Americans were facing was the frightening loss of control over our lives. As a leader, you need to be aware that, in your heart, you have known this all along. The most difficult thing about losing control is finally accepting it.

My husband, Gunter, and I faced the issue of loss of control many times during the maiden voyage of *Pacific Bliss*. At the out-set—even before we left the Catana factory in Canet, France—we had to change schedules and delay crew arrivals until our yacht was ready to make the passage safely. When we finally left to cross the Mediterranean, the winds and waves from a Force 10 storm forced us to take refuge in Estartit, Spain, the very first night. Months later, off the coast of Colombia, we were actually caught in a Force 10 storm, with 53-knot winds pushing us along like a toy at 25 knots! It was like being on a roller-coaster ride that didn't end in two minutes.

As if there were bookends, Voyage One ended with our being out of control again—months behind our original plans—as we beat our way up the long coastlines of Central America, Mexico, and Baja. Even Hurricane Adolf, which churned 250 miles south of us when we were in Puerto Vallarta, delayed our crossing of the Sea of Cortez. We were again delayed in Cabo San Lucas and in Turtle Bay, waiting for seas to calm. By the end of the voyage, we had calmly accepted being out of control. There are no guarantees in life. The dangers can be terrorists, pirates—or simply the raging seas.

There is a certain peace in being out of control. It reminds one of how much there is to lose—and how fast one can lose it.

As a leader, you may be responsible for the bottom line of your company or department, you may control promotions and dis-missals, and you may begin to think of yourself as the center of the universe. Nature has the awesome power to put things back in per-spective. Events outside our control can be Nature's way of telling us to experience life and to work in a calmer, less stressful way. You reach an acceptance, and you learn to control that which is within your power to do so. You also accept the fact that uncontrollable external forces may intrude, and you will have to wait out the ensuing storm.

# # #

Lois Joy Crandell Hofmann, CEO emeritus of Genetronics, Inc., serves on boards of industry and charitable organizations, such as BioCom San Diego and UCSD Cancer Center. During her leadership of Genetronics, she took the company from a valuation of $750,000 to over $100 million in market capitalization. Lois also invented the "Crandell Catheter," with two patents granted and several more pending.

Previous to Genetronics, Lois held leadership positions with several large companies, including Medtronic, Inc., and Control Data Corporation.

Since her retirement, Lois has been circumnavigating the world with her husband in their forty-three-foot yacht, *Pacific Bliss*.

Thriving on Change

Terry Swack

In 1993, TSDesign was an eight-year-old strategic communications and graphic design firm. Over the previous five years, the advent of personal computers and desktop publishing had dramatically changed the landscape of the design profession. Anyone with a computer could now call himself or herself a graphic designer. That, in combination with a terrible recession, had put me on a quest to search for what I would do next.

In March of that year, my technology mentor showed me Mosaic—a piece of free software used to view this new thing called the World Wide Web—and asked if I would help him put some information into cyberspace. He asked me, a designer—not a technologist—to help, because everything already there looked so bad. At the time, the browser technology was so simple that there wasn't much design one could do, but knowledge of good typography and information design made a difference in presenting content effectively.

Over the following year, I hired a director of technology, and I acquired e-mail and Internet access for each computer at TSDesign. We did some pro bono work and some paying work, making inroads in important places. A number of employees didn't like or understand the work and chose to leave the company. This work required a range of different kinds of people, and most importantly, people who understood the need for collaboration rather than individual contribution only. While I didn't expressly reengineer the company, the natural attrition had the same effect.

By 1994, I had decided I would devote the firm to humanizing technology by taking a lead in designing how people would experience the Web. Since there were no designers doing this, no one could say whether the way I was doing it was right or wrong. It also meant there was no competition yet, which allowed us a head start in making a name in this space.

By 1995, TSDesign had become an Internet strategy and product design firm. In 1996, the development of the User Experience Audit (SM) was the first offering of its kind, and it positioned TSDesign as the industry leader in design analysis and user experience management. Clients ranged from Fortune 500 companies to dot-coms, including 3M, Compaq, Dell, BankBoston, Cendant Mortgage, WebCriteria, Tripod and PlanetAll. In December 1999, I sold TSDesign to Razorfish, a global digital services provider.

I can't take credit for having a vision in those early days of what the Web would become. However, I had the understanding of its capabilities and the belief that design can make technology more accessible to people and make a difference in their lives. These two things gave me the strength and determination to go down that road and stay the course.

# # #

Terry Swack, twenty-plus-year veteran of the graphic design profession and a leading digital strategist, was founder and CEO of TSDesign, an Internet strategy and product design firm, later acquired by Razorfish, a global digital services provider. As vice president of experience design, she was a principal strategist in the redesign of the Razorfish worldwide service delivery organization.

The development of the User Experience Audit was the first offering of its kind and positioned TSDesign as an industry leader in Web design analysis and user experience management.

Terry now consults independently, serves on the American Institute of Graphic Arts (AIGA) board of directors, is the AIGA Experience Design community of interest co-founder and national chair, and is a contributing reviewer to *Internet World's Deconstructing*.

Passionate Leadership

Maggie Rogers

Leadership was thrust upon me—I did not welcome it, look for it, or even desire it. Goodness knows, I never even identified it as such until quite recently, and then mostly because others have insisted that I have it. Most of my life, I have hidden from it and tried not to show myself as I am. My fear? That I would be told I was "too big for my boots"—a constant refrain meted out to me in my childhood and growing years. I have been terrified that I would "go too far" and hurt or upset somebody if I showed that I knew what I knew. It was much better, I thought, to let myself be hurt and upset. After all, I was "big enough" to cope, wasn't I?

I have always been afraid to "be" and have actively (though unconsciously) pushed away the very clear indicators of the leadership qualities others saw in me. Apparently they could see what I did not yet see in myself and wanted, in spite of that, to be part of my team.

Thinking back on it, I can see that by primary school, the signs were already beginning to show and, by intermediate and then high school, I was unstoppable. I was leader of the junior and senior choirs at school. At church, I was the deputy leader of the girls' choir (the only girls' choir in all of New Zealand), and the youngest alto in the senior choir. I was the chair or president of the Friday night Bible class and on the debating team in Form 3 (instead of five years later!). My most surprising achievement was that of being elected captain of Hodges House during my stay at Palmerston North Girls High School. The reason that this was surprising to me was that it was essentially a sports' captaincy. I was and am no sportswoman! The high jump, the long jump, and any other jumps defeated me then and still do now! Why on earth did my fellow pupils vote for me to lead them? It remains a mystery but by golly, we did do well that year.

I had decided in Form 3 that I wanted to be "head girl" in my final year at high school. I worked hard to achieve that goal. I was offered the position, refused it, left school early, and went off to university where I failed miserably at first. Why did I do it? Because I was afraid that at the end of the year, when the head girl had to make a speech in front of the whole school, the teachers and parents, I would cry. In those days, I was so ashamed of my tears. It didn't occur to me to question this until years later when my wonderful supervisor, Tom Ormay, told me that it is okay to cry. I knew I was going to have to say good-bye to a patient prematurely and was afraid I would cry in the final session. Tom said, "Maybe it's all right if you cry, Maggie. We do when we say good-bye to someone we love. Perhaps you will let your patient see what he meant to you, and that may be an important gift that you give him. He will see that he has been valuable to you." Since then, I have never looked back. You can be emotional and still be a leader! You don't have to give your power away. You do have to speak up, and others do need to find you in your words. It took me a long time to learn to speak in my own voice and to be accountable for my words and actions. I'm still working on it, and I suspect it's the work of a lifetime.

I have always been passionate about everything in life. My friends always want to know what I'm up to—now. I always have some new scheme on the go. What I enjoy most of all is the way my friends and colleagues seem to get fired up by the latest thing I am involved in and come along with me for the ride. My friends commonly say that they love being around me because I enjoy life so much. They tell me they feel I bring such a lot to their lives because of my enthusiasm, passion, and willingness to be open about where I am in any given situation. I remain amazed that I am blessed with wonderful friends who want to be with me. What pleasure!

"The Online Center of Excellence (OCE): excellence creators" is my latest passion. My life's work has been helping people to solve problems for themselves, not by themselves, through the therapeutic enterprise. My fields are therapy and education—first as a classroom teacher, then university lecturer and, more recently, co-directing my own training association— The Psychotherapy and Hypnosis Training Association—in conjunction with my co-director and friend, Sylvia Wright. We established a center of excellence in a field where standards were lacking.

Then along came the Internet and I realized that I could either ignore it or attend to its development, both personally and professionally. Having developed a studio gallery, I decided to practice using the Internet by putting the gallery on-line. In addition to being an opportunity to learn, it was great fun. My fantasies about artists turned out to be not quite accurate, so it was time for the next idea to come into being. Why not offer therapy and continuing professional education on-line? And why not look at how this might interest the business-to-business market? Hence OCE was formed.

What is my dream? I want each and every person who is suffering or in great pain to have someone to talk to when they need to talk. Those dark nights of the soul spent all alone are almost unbearable. I want people to learn that they can solve their problems for themselves wherever they may be, but that they don't have to do so by themselves; hence the 24/7, 365-days-a-year provision. I want people to be able to explore being the very best they can be within a supportive, friendly place, with someone who is really there for them. I want people, who want to be better personally and professionally, who may not need therapy but who do need support, to find good quality coaching to help them achieve their dreams. Finally, I want therapists and coaches to continue to learn, think, talk, evaluate, and become better and better. I want them to be able to really understand this new medium of working, grasp it, use it, grow with it, and enjoy it. Because of this, there is a continuing professional education and development component in the business.

I am now two years, four months into the project. I had given away leadership of it for eighteen months. Without me at the helm, the business foundered, and I finally decided that I'd better take control of the company. We are going from strength to strength, with the launch and development of the U. K. company completed and now the development of the U. S. subsidiary just completed. The company will be financially successful within a short time. In every other way, we are already excellence creators. Again I am blessed with a most wonderful team, led in the U. S. by Dr. Steven Gans, a man of great wisdom, who enjoys working with me and I with him.

What moves me most is how much I love getting up every day and working towards making my dream come true. Work is so often play for me. It is challenging, creative, and sometimes downright difficult—and I love it! I wouldn't have it any other way. To be engaged in doing what I am most passionate about is a true gift and makes life worth living. To have others who want to be part of my dream adds to that pleasure. Perhaps this is what leadership is all about.

# # #

Maggie Rogers is the London-based chief executive officer of "Online Center of Excellence: excellence creators," a global company providing personal therapy, corporate and personal stress coaching, and continuing professional education and development for therapists and coaches. She is a psychoanalytic psychotherapist and hypnotherapist by training and also an educator. Maggie has traveled widely and has lived in a number of countries including South Africa, New Zealand, India, Nepal, and the United Kingdom.

Survival Skills Lead to Achievement

Karen Carter

Adversity can open the doors to new challenges and careers and can help us achieve more than we had ever imagined. It can also show our loved ones the possibilities for themselves and can encourage them to reach for new stars in their own lives.

This type of dynamic experience happened in my life. For several years, I had been working two jobs, one for the United States Post Office and the other for a casualty insurance agency. My first clients in the insurance business were loggers and part of the Apache Indian tribe. It was fascinating to work with men, who had never worked with a woman who knew anything about their logging equipment and trucks. Also, it was sometimes difficult for me to relate to people when I stood eye-to-eye with their belt buckles. However, it didn't take long for them to realize that I did know much about their equipment and how to rate it, and that I had knowledge about the type of insurance coverage they needed.

I enjoyed working with the Apaches. When they needed a loan for their first insurance premium, I took a chance and loaned them the money. As I was the sole support of three children, this was quite a risk; however, they always paid me back with both money and loyalty.

I then became licensed in the life insurance part of the business. Although company representatives tried to discourage me, I studied every book I could find on the topic. The more I was told that a woman could not make it in the insurance business, the more determined I became that I would be successful.

About a year later, I decided to move to the "big city" of Phoenix, Arizona, to give my daughters the opportunity to explore the theater, music, and lifestyle that was not available in small towns. After continuing to work for the U.S. Post Office in Phoenix for six months, I wanted to try my hand at real estate. I thought this might be similar to the insurance business that I had enjoyed previously. After going to real estate classes and getting my license, I sold my first business during the first month. I received the largest paycheck I had ever seen, and I was on top of the world!

That world was shattered with just one sneeze! Something in my back had gone out, and the next day, in agony, I wasn't able to get home from the office because of severe pain in my legs. I went to a chiropractor, who turned out to be the wrong doctor for me. It was discovered that he had crushed two discs in my back. Two days later, I had a leg that I was unable to move, a turned-in foot, and an 85 percent chance that I would never walk again without a leg brace.

Major back surgery and six months of learning to walk again changed the course of my life. I had been in commercial real estate, and the economy had taken a major downturn during the six months that I had not been working. I saw no future for me in this field at the time, so I started replying to ads in the newspaper. One of these ads happened to be placed by a major life insurance company. Since I felt I was so far down financially, physically, and emotionally, I knew I had no place to go but up and decided to give it my all. I had no choice but to swim, because I couldn't afford to sink.

Upon achieving an increasing degree of success with this major life insurance corporation, I was invited to their home office for a conference with sixteen other women. All sixteen of these women were high achievers like myself. The leaders of the company wanted to learn what made us successful when others were not. At the time, there were only 150 women in sales positions with the company nationally, and the company was realizing that we women were doing better than the men. They wanted to know why.

We met in Boston for four days and combined our knowledge of success and life experience to find a common bond. The outstanding thread was that each of us, except for one, had faced a devastating experience that would have ended the careers of almost anyone. One woman was married to a U-2 pilot who had crashed and was missing. A year later, her only child died. Another had been abandoned by her husband and left alone with several children, one of them disabled. I myself had become paralyzed, almost lost the use of my leg, had fought to learn to walk again, and was the sole support of my three children. I overcame the disability, because I couldn't see myself rearing my children from a wheelchair. For each of us, our experiences had made the cement that held us above the average and made us not only survivors, but also high achievers.

I was the first woman hired in six years by my office of this insurance company. At that time, they didn't even have a gender-neutral aptitude test. I didn't know until a year later that my general agent had paid my salary out of his own pocket, because my doctor wouldn't give me clearance to work full time. Can you imagine someone having that much confidence in me in my condition at the time? He could see something that I couldn't. Several years later, I learned that he had suffered a heart attack at age thirty-one and had opted not to sit and watch the world go by. He had become very successful. That's the survival instinct again.

Not long ago, I met a woman who exuded self-confidence and radiated love to everyone she saw. Her background was quite similar to the women in that conference that I had attended several years ago. She had been through several unsuccessful marriages, a devastating automobile accident, and financial problems. She had decided that she wasn't down for the count, and she has achieved so much more than she had ever imagined possible.

The wonderful thing that happens to determined women is that it mysteriously rubs off on their children and others they love. My

children have been in the trenches with me, and they are high achievers. They say it was the way they were reared. As women, our
daughters and granddaughters have taken the opening we have made
by finally obtaining the key to the executive washroom. They have
seen the realm of endless possibilities for themselves and those to
follow. For me, that makes every inch worth the battle.

# # #

Karen Carter, a native Arizonan, has been in the casualty, personal
property, and life insurance fields for more than thirty years. Before
opening Carter Insurance and Pension Services in 1985, she led the
Arizona agency of a major life insurance firm in production. She
holds a Chartered Life Underwriters degree and a Chartered Financial Consultants degree. Karen is a nationally recognized
motivational speaker, as well as a private trust administrator and is
very active in community affairs.

You *Do* Have a Choice!

Robin M. Muscia

On July 17, 1996, I ended a dysfunctional existence that I had created for myself. That was the day I started a 2,500-mile journey to the glorious state of Arizona to achieve independence once again.

The moment I realized I would be free of my painful surroundings was when I stood in front of my mother's apartment and saw my automobile packed with just the necessities. For the first time, I could breathe easier knowing I would not have to face another day in a living hell. I am happy to say this was my choice. Yes, I now realize that everything one does in life, as well as every decision one makes, is a choice!

I remained in an abusive marriage for nearly ten years. My ex-husband was an alcoholic and one of the "good old boys" on the police force where we lived. I tried very hard to keep the marriage intact; however, as time went on, it became more and more difficult. All the nurturing in the world could not save the relationship. I struggled with my ex-husband's unacceptable behaviors, which included burning down our home, losing his driver's license to drunk driving, and living with a deflated ego because he was demoted to desk work. I finally realized I was definitely a victim of domestic violence. The most shocking episode was when he threatened me with his gun one Sunday morning. I was having a telephone conversation with my mother when he suddenly appeared before my eyes with a revolver. My mother later told me that I screamed through the phone like someone was killing me. She ran out of the house in her pajamas, jumped into her car, and drove to my home. She found me in a fetal position in the corner of my dining room. I was in shock and totally speechless. She put me in the car and drove me to the hospital emergency room. I remained in the hospital for more than a week.

Without doubt, I was a part of the "power and control" cycle. There are eight pieces to this cycle: emotional abuse, isolation, denying and blaming, using children, economic abuse, intimidation, coercion and threats, and male privilege—"master of the castle syndrome." I learned that women need to take a step back, and make a checklist to ensure they are not caught up in this vicious pattern of abuse in any way. I had been an expert at hiding my problems: no one, not even my own family, ever knew the challenges I was facing.

I often would ask myself, "What is wrong with me? I am an intelligent woman with a good career and a lot going for me, so why am I continuing with life in this way?" Because this man, who was my husband at the time, had many connections with the judicial system, I always felt there was no way out. Finally, after one of his tirades, I looked at the shattered pieces of my "Precious Moments" figurines, which had been thrown throughout the house, and I ran to the telephone and called the police. That was both the end and the beginning.

During the next several months, my health suffered terribly from the constant stress. I was diagnosed with lupus and fibromyalgia. I moved in with my mother, because I was bedridden for almost three months. My body had broken down so badly I could not walk, stand, or even roll over in bed without experiencing excruciating pain. During my seven-month stay with my mother, my ex-husband was constantly stalking me, and I received no help from the local police. Finally, my family and I met with the Victim Witness Protection department and the head prosecutor to discuss my situation. The recommendation from the prosecutor's office was to move out of the state.

I arrived in Phoenix, Arizona, on July 22, 1996. I had traveled with my seventy-year-old godmother, and we shared an apartment together. Since I had no bed, I slept on the floor. When I left my two homes in the eastern part of the country, material items were not at the top of my priority list! My health and state of mind were much more important to me.

Although I have always been a Christian, I pray even more since surviving this abusive relationship. Every day when I pray, I refer to two books from my mother: *Joy for the Journey: A Woman's Book of Joyful Promises* and *Positive Prayers for Power-Filled Living*. These books are with me at all times.

Because I had a twenty-year medical background, I was able to obtain a position at the Mayo Clinic within two weeks of my arrival in Phoenix. As I continued to grow and rebuild my life, I felt the heaviness lifting out of my heart. I was a *survivor* of domestic violence. Many women are not this fortunate. Although I wanted to talk with victims and encourage them in some way, I found I was still too emotional at that time in my life.

Today, I am proud to say, at age forty, I returned to school for continuing education in business and communications. I am the president of Speakers Academy, a marketing, training and development company I co-founded, which is located in North Scottsdale. I am married to a brilliant man who has supported me in so many ways. I have an incredible twenty-one-year-old daughter, who is in college. The health issues are in remission. During my time here in Arizona, I have connected with so many wonderful people and organizations. Now that the healing process is almost completed, I am now able to speak to domestic violence victims and volunteer my time at a child abuse shelter. It is important for me to give back. I went through this crisis for a reason, and now I need to give inspiration to those who need some help. Sometimes I am amazed at what I have accomplished in a short period of time, and I am excited to think what remarkable things are still in store for me along the way.

Since my journey across the country, I have worked diligently on acquiring and maintaining the leadership qualities and behaviors that have helped me become successful, both in my business and in my personal life. These include:

- Count your blessings.
- Take time for meditation or spiritual readings during the day.
- Respect yourself and others.
- Face your fears head on.
- Trust yourself.
- Motivate yourself.
- Discipline yourself.
- Choose to have a positive attitude.
- Be patient with yourself and others.
- Celebrate the victories you have accomplished.
- Learn as much as you can, as you can never stop learning.
- Listen.
- Laugh often.
- Read.
- Focus on your mission.
- Don't be afraid to dream.
- Visualize your thoughts.
- Write your thoughts and dreams down on paper; you will be surprised how many come true!
- Have a plan for your life.
- Ask yourself, "What are my priorities?"
- Be persistent. If you fall down, get back up!
- Dare to risk. If you don't try, you will live in the unknown forever.
- If ever there is a mountain in front of you, figure out a way to go over it or through it. Never let the mountain stop you!

I hope you will believe in yourself as much as I have believed in myself. My inner strength came through when I needed it most.

Over the past few years, I have come to recognize qualities in myself that I never knew existed. Life has become fascinating!

You can truly turn your life around if you make the choice to do so!

# # #

Robin M. Muscia is a co-founder and president of Speakers Academy, Inc. As a professional speaker with more than twenty years of sales and management experience, she consults with business professionals on marketing, networking, and image development through public speaking. Robin has received awards from the Arizona Small Business Association for her efforts in helping promote small businesses in Arizona. In addition, she is active in providing support and assistance for women and children who are victims of domestic violence. Robin can be contacted by e-mail at Rmuscia@speakersacademy.net.

Heroism and Leadership

Sara Arbel

Leadership is a subject that has been covered and explored from all angles possible; yet we continue to look at it as if we might find some new insight, some new definition, or some new perspective.

As I am sitting here at midnight on a moonless night in Tel Aviv, Israel, I find myself wondering how I could best contribute to this much-discussed subject. The quiet night and the silence of the sky are so much in contrast to the firing and battles of the day, as if the two sides take their rest before the next battle. It is sad that each family here has had three generations of soldiers fighting our wars. Each generation brought hopes for peace, hopes that they will not know the smell of gunpowder, and hopes that peace and mutual freedom will be the rulers of their lives.

Sometimes, I wonder if the bloodshed would continue on like this if the leaders of the two sides were women, if the leaders had to bear the babies, breastfeed them and protect them until an age where they could let them go. Would they let go of them to die in the battlefields? I wonder if a Palestinian mother and an Israeli mother would work out an earlier settlement of a peace agreement, if they would build universities, if they would grow fields of organic food, if they would develop the land, and if they would invest in culture and education. In peace, there is no need for boundaries to be guarded by soldiers. In peace, there is no need to invest in guns and war weapons. In peace, there is an opportunity for freedom and prosperity for all.

As I am sitting here daydreaming on this calm night, I know that our reality is that the leaders of the region will continue to use the weapons of war, and the mothers of the two sides will continue to bury their sons.

When I was a young girl, I had this fantasy of being a leader, one associated with heroism. Being a daughter of a partisan and a fighter of the Warsaw ghetto uprising, I have heard many heroic stories about my father. Everyone called him a hero, and he received a very high medal of honor from the Polish government for his heroic actions in saving 400 people during the war. He hid the people in the woods and brought food to their hiding places. My father was a hero, but was he a leader? He was not a leader in the sense of holding a torch for people to follow. He was not a charismatic man, and he was very humble and quiet, never bragging about his past. In fact, I first learned about my father's heroism long after it all happened. It was just by coincidence, while living in Montreal, when an old man there asked me for my maiden name. When I told him, he inquired about my father's name and origin, and, from that moment, he couldn't stop telling me about him, how he was searching for him all these years, about the fact that my father saved his life and the lives of his entire family. That was the first time I ever heard of the 400 people he saved. My father paid a high price for not disclosing the hiding places of the Jews. The SS killed his wife and two children, and he himself was tortured, lost an eye, and was shot in the legs and chest.

My father never wanted the praise and the fame he could have received. As I analyze this now, I know he was a hero, but not necessarily a leader. He definitely challenged the status quo, and his goal was to save many people from the hands of the Nazis. He definitely had his set of values and priorities well focused, but he was not a visionary. I am not sure if he planned one step beyond the one he took at each moment.

I believe that leaders are born out of conflicting sets of needs that are being expressed by groups of people. Leaders recognize these needs and are driven to satisfy them. If it's wartime, economic upheaval, famine, environmental tragedies, or threat of any kind to large groups of people, leaders recognize the needs and move forward to satisfy these needs. On the other hand, they also recognize the needs and take action at times when prosperity requires direction, organizations require structure, overflow of information requires prioritization, etc. Different times, conditions, and realities require different leaders with different sets of values and standards.

I believe that some leaders will emerge and even surprise themselves at the moment of crisis and need. Often, leaders discover themselves in the process of leadership.

Today, when I look back at my own life, I can recognize some threads of my father's legacy to me. I set standards and coach people to achieve their goals and visions. In many venues, I am a pioneer as I seek new challenges and communicate my vision to others.

One does not have to be a hero in order to lead. That kind of leadership might be long gone, but I still find it so romantic. Why not dare to dream of this kind of leadership?

# # #

Sara Arbel, who lives in Israel, is a business and high-achiever coach with clients in several countries. She has owned an art gallery, an image and design company, and a consulting company. Sara has also served as an officer in the Israeli army, specializing in crisis management of civilians. Her passion is supporting individuals to achieve significant results.

Dare to Wear Your Red Shoes

Marion Lonn

When you grow up the eleventh of eleven children in a rural community in Saskatchewan, Canada, the options for your future can appear to be limited. While many of my friends and family have had very fulfilling lives staying close to this environment, a few of us were determined to venture away. We dared to be different.

Today, I am vice president of Internal Audit for Levi Strauss & Company, and my journey to this position has been far from direct. I started my career as a market research analyst. If I had to give one key to summarize how I have achieved career growth and managed the changes in my career, I would say I did it by taking careful risks and not fearing change. Couple this with setting goals, having dreams, and using all of your life experiences in fulfilling your responsibilities, and success can be yours.

About goals and risks . . . About having a dream

I very clearly knew from a young age that I *was* going to attend university. Growing up in a small farm community in the late sixties, it wasn't a given that even a good student would go past high school. Besides, my father wasn't all that supportive of post-secondary education for many of my older brothers and sisters. His outlook started to change with my brother, who was four years older than I, and my sister, who was two years older. That was only step one. Knowing that I wanted my life to be different, I looked for nontraditional things to study—not teaching, not nursing, and not home economics. I went to business school, which in those days had a male/female ratio of 95/5, not the 50/50 ratio one sees today.

Along with taking risks came the willingness to deal with change, which can come in many different forms.

In 1982, my husband, Harvey, and I moved from Edmonton to Toronto with Levi Strauss Canada. It was at a time when the two subsidiaries of the company were consolidating, and I was one of the fortunate few who were asked to relocate. Before this relocation, Harvey had a position in the computer industry, and I had started to interview for other positions in Edmonton. One of these interviews had even resulted in a job offer. We sat down, each of us taking a piece of paper and writing down all the plusses and minuses of moving and of staying put. Making the decision to move was an extremely difficult process. However, it set a pattern that we used many times over the coming years. We have since moved with the company to England, to Brussels, and to San Francisco. These decisions never became easier to make. In many ways, it became more difficult as our children grew and as the implications for Harvey's career became greater. However, we have made each of the decisions thoughtfully. We try to understand what we are likely to gain and what we are likely to lose. Moving to San Francisco was probably one of the most difficult decisions, because we realized it would have a profound impact on our children's lives. They were nine and twelve at the time, and we knew that it would have a significant impact on their identity as Canadians. Thanks to our decision-making process, it turned out to be a good move for the family.

About being your best . . . About learning . . . About using what you know

Early in my career, our division general manager said that most new employees would give you about 85 percent of what you had expected. I have always learned as much as I can about the business and about what is going on around me, and I use that knowledge as

I move into new positions. I share that knowledge with those on my team. That knowledge may have come from having helped prepare jeans at our factory in Edmonton for a fit test; from having worked in marketing research, as well as in finance and in different geographic locations; from knowing people; from remembering why changes were made in the past; and from understanding some of the intricacies of what makes the company work. Sharing this knowledge helps make the individuals on the team more effective, and ultimately that benefits the group as a whole.

However, as I think back on my career, I realize that there were many times when I didn't have the right balance between hard work for the company and looking out for my own development. I remember when I was working at the European Headquarters in Brussels, and the company was doing group process training. It was September, which would have been a great time for a week in the Belgian countryside, but there were many different projects that just had to be completed, so I did not attend. This is just one example of the pattern I had developed. Not so long ago, I decided, "Enough!" The amazing thing is that I received two benefits—the learning from the training and the improved perception of others because I participated in the training. It said that I listened and that I cared about improving my capabilities.

There is something else I've learned related to personal development—I now stick up for myself and ask for resources to help me. Moving to internal audit meant that I would have a lot to learn in order to be successful. So, when I said yes, I also said, "Here is what I need." I have had access to both a personal and a professional coach for the past year, and this has helped me tremendously. My coach, Yvonne, is tremendously helpful in encouraging me, asking just the right question to keep me focused on my goals, and prodding me to do what isn't always comfortable. My other coach, Scott, has been a great sounding board and gives me the courage to lead my staff of seasoned auditors into new ways of approaching work and reaching for higher goals. Attending seminars has allowed me to gain professional credibility with my team. They are now accustomed to hearing, "Watch out! I now know more about what I don't know."

About making a difference . . . About creating a picture of a new future

When I look back on the positions I've had, I can really feel that I have made a difference. When I moved to the United Kingdom, the department there was quite traditional, and people had been doing things the same way for a long time. We physically moved the financial people closer to the marketing and sales people, so that the financial people could provide more insights, be more influential, and, through this, become better contributors to business success. In Brussels, a colleague and I led a team to redefine the roles and expectations for the European finance organization. I didn't accept my current position to maintain the status quo, nor was this expected. In the past year, we have created a three-year plan to move a good department to *greatness*. My advice to the people working for me is, "Don't stand still. If you do, you are losing ground, because everything around you *is* moving forward!"

About change and attitude

Not surprisingly, during my twenty-plus years with Levi Strauss, I have been through many ups and downs, periods of consolidation and layoffs, and numerous reorganizations. Through all of this, I sometimes wonder why certain people have survived and why others haven't. Although no company ever makes perfect decisions during these times, I see a theme from what I have observed and practiced. Leaders don't appreciate whiners, and they don't like people who don't want to be part of the team. When change was happening, I have always made choices and decisions as to whether or not I could "live with" the changes. The new CFO arrived a year after I moved to the United States, and he initiated a review of the efficiency and effectiveness of the U. S. finance organization. One of the results was the creation of a Shared Services Center in Eugene, Oregon, and some of my department responsibilities would be relocated. I had to decide if I could "live with" the new direction. The secret was to do my homework, say my piece, and then make my own personal decisions. However, leaders sometimes have to fight for their beliefs. Initially, a particular role was slated to be relocated to Eugene, and I felt very strongly that the consultants, who were making the recommendation, had "gotten it wrong." I put forward arguments to key people. I argued from the perspective of what is best for the company and not what is best for Marion Lonn. The role is still here.

About using all you know

I see many parallels between being a mother of two boys (now thirteen and sixteen) and being a leader of a work group. At work, I use what I have learned from being a mother. Some of this has come from one particular book about child rearing, *Children the Challenge* by Rudolf Dreikurs, which is about treating children with respect and equality, and about teaching them responsibility through understanding consequences. I dare to be a little bit crazy at home. I also dare to have fun at work and to be energetic. It helps to develop a spirit of camaraderie in my team and allows me to always be "human" and to show humility. This makes the tough times and tough conversations easier.

About being yourself . . . About being confident . . . About wearing your red shoes

About two years ago, I went shopping at Nordstrom's and found the most wonderful pair of red shoes. They were one of the newest styles from Cole Haan with open toes and open backs. They were a very rich red, which bled into black towards the edges. I *had* to have them! It was a special treat after a long period of stress at work. At the time, I was involved in helping the Levi Strauss Americas Leadership Team develop the strategic plan, and there were a lot of new players on the team. The new CEO was serving as president for the Americas, and the CFO was temporarily managing the supply chain.

My boss, the vice president of marketing services, and I would plan the group sessions, which I would lead. Gradually, I started to feel more comfortable and my confidence grew to the point that I had the courage to wear those red shoes. When someone made a comment, I could be myself, kick up my heels a bit, and say, "Yes! Aren't they great shoes?" These red shoes symbolize me being myself—a woman, a wife, a mother, and a successful career person!

# # #

During her twenty-four-year career with Levi Strauss & Company, Marion Lonn has held leadership positions in Canada, United Kingdom, Belgium, and the United States. Her multifunctional responsibilities have spanned from marketing planning to financial management to internal auditing. Marion led the Levi Strauss Americas Planning and Performance group and is vice president of Internal Audit.

Section III

Set Powerful Goals!

Set Powerful Goals!

Although leaders are visionaries and dreamers, they are also stable and goal-oriented. As Harvey Mackay cited, "A goal is a dream with a deadline." Leaders have written goals. They communicate their goals, visualize the results, and reward themselves and others for the accomplishment of milestones.

When she was six years old, Elizabeth Blackwell already had a major goal, that of doing something "hard" when she grew up. Still quite young when her father died, she began teaching in order to assist the family financially. While she was engaged in the teaching profession, she was able to further define the goal she had set at age six. She decided to become a doctor of medicine. Her challenge was that there had never been a female doctor, as women were not admitted to medical school.

In 1847, Elizabeth focused on pursuing her goal by applying to medical schools. Application after application was rejected until she applied to Geneva Medical School in Geneva, New York. It was there that the administrator asked the students to decide whether to admit her. The students, believing this was a practical joke, endorsed her admission.

Both students and townspeople were horrified when they learned that Elizabeth was serious. Her life became extremely difficult as she was ridiculed and kept from classroom medical

91

demonstrations. However, Elizabeth was persistent, and the other students eventually became impressed with her ability. She graduated at the top of her class in 1849. She was the first woman to graduate from medical school and became the first female doctor of medicine in the modern era.

Elizabeth faced additional challenges when an eye infection left her blind in one eye. Hospitals refused her association, and landlords would not rent her office space to set up a private practice. However, she was committed to her goal and bought a house in which to begin her practice.

Dr. Elizabeth Blackwell's accomplishments in the field of medicine are many. They include establishing the New York Infirmary for Women and Children, becoming the first woman to have her name on the British medical register, organizing the Women's Central Association of Relief, opening the Women's Medical College, organizing the Women's Health Society in England, founding the London School of Medicine for Women, being appointed professor of gynecology at the London School of Medicine for Children, and writing and publishing six books. All of this started with a powerful goal.

These tips will help you to set and achieve powerful goals:

1. **Before setting a goal, think about what you *really* want in your life.** Many of us set goals to do what we think we *should* do; however, we do not want the results enough to remain committed to the goal.

2. **Ask yourself if your goal is in alignment with your priorities in life.** When a person's goals and priorities are not in alignment, a sense of being overwhelmed, or inertia, can stand in the way of accomplishing the goals.

3. **Ensure that your goal is realistic and achievable.** Many people give up on trying to reach their goal, because they were hoping to achieve the impossible when they set the goal. However, it is also important to engage in possibility thinking and to realize that you are capable of achieving what others might consider impossible. Give your goal some "stretch."

4. **Clearly state your goal** by describing your desired results exactly as you wish them to be. State the goal in terms of what will be accomplished and when it will be accomplished.

5. **Ensure that your goal is measurable** by asking yourself how you will know whether you have achieved this goal.

6. **Write your goal** on paper, and keep this piece of paper in a place where you can look at it every day. Fewer than 3 percent of all adults have written goals, and research shows that people with written goals are more likely to achieve them.

7. **Make a commitment to yourself to reach the goal**, ensuring that you understand the effort that will be involved in doing this.

8. **Visualize the end result.** Close your eyes, and create a mental movie of how the end result will look. In this mental movie, visualize yourself enjoying these results. Repeat this visualization daily, picturing yourself as if you have already achieved your goal. In this section, Vicki Tolman ("Aligning Dreams and Goals for Success") discusses how goal setting and visualization techniques helped to fulfill her dreams of earning the use of a car and advancing very quickly to a leadership position in her Mary Kay cosmetics business.

9. **Describe the benefits of your goal.** Do this on paper, so that you can read the benefits whenever you might struggle with doing the things needed to reach the goal.

10. **Establish milestones as mini-goals**, and write them down as well. It is easier to work on one small step at a time than on a big goal.

11. **Develop and implement an action plan.** Determine the steps that you will take to achieve your goal, and write these down.

12. **Communicate your goal** to supportive people who might be able to contribute to its achievement, either through direct efforts or through encouragement.

13. **Reward yourself as you reach milestones** along the way to achieving your goal. By giving recognition to ourselves for our accomplishments, we expand our enthusiasm and energy to accomplish more.

14. **Remain flexible.** Although you will set a date for accomplishing your goal, there could be an emergency situation that you need to handle en route. When taking care of this situation is a higher priority than the goal, allow yourself to adjust your schedule for accomplishing the goal. Also, as you achieve your goals, you may change direction and will, of course, set new goals for yourself. In this section, Marilyn Straka ("On the Level") tells about the goals she set and achieved at various times in her life and discusses her newest business—San Francisco walking tours without hills.

15. **If you make a mistake, give yourself permission to start again.** We are all in a constant process of growth and development. We can use our mistakes as learning opportunities and become even stronger than we had been previously.

All of the women featured in this book have powerful goals, which continue to contribute to their effectiveness as leaders. Your goals, integrated with your dreams, will enhance your success as a leader.

On the Level

Marilyn Straka

"On The Level" is the name of my walking tour business in hilly San Francisco! I have designed tours of neighborhoods and parks that avoid the hills and steps—making the tours accessible to everyone, even to those using wheelchairs and walkers or pushing a stroller. But that is the end of my story. Let me start at the beginning. I want to tell you about some guidelines I follow that will have a positive effect on your life. I want to "level" with you on how you, too, can have a dream and make that dream come true.

My definition of success has changed as I have moved through the different stages of my life:

- As a child and teenager—overcoming extreme shyness
- As a young adult—raising my son as a single parent, without help from his father
- As a mature adult—achieving a level in my computer-based career where I enjoy my work and earn a substantial salary that meets my needs
- My current stage—developing my "On The Level" idea into a thriving small business and serving on nonprofit boards to benefit the community

The social part of getting through school was a major challenge, as I was extremely shy. My mother realized the depth of my insecurity when I admitted the reason I could not go to school alone was that "I may not be able to get the door open." Solving a deep-seated problem like this took many small steps. Since I could not see people clearly, getting glasses was one step. Later, transitioning to contact lenses boosted my self-esteem. Still later, I realized that it was *fun* to talk with people. Today I actually enjoy speaking to groups, thanks to an excellent class I took many years ago on making effective presentations. Recently I saw my instructor standing at the bus stop. I recognized him—after twenty-five years—and stopped to express my thanks. I've learned that everyone loves to be acknowledged. Today, most people do not believe that I once was very shy, but inside I know. I still have to push myself to reach out and initiate a conversation—knowing the rewards will be greater than the risk.

As I reflect on my successes—raising my son, reaching my thirty-year career goals, and serving on boards—I realize they have a lot in common. They are all projects that I have managed using the guidelines that direct my life. These guidelines and ideas are not new. Although I may give them a different twist, you have probably heard of them before. However, I've learned that it takes hearing an idea seven times to make it one's own. I have two guides that keep me on the right track: Norman Vincent Peale's *The Power of Positive Thinking* and Joan Gustafson's *A Woman Can Do That!* Following are the guidelines I use for success:

Determine what you do well, and capitalize on that.
It is realistic to assume that you are not good at everything. Are you good at working with people, or do you work better alone? Are you a take-action person, or do you come up with great ideas for others to implement? Are you detail-oriented, or do you see the big picture better? You can share your skills and partner with others who have complementary skills.

Develop three messages.
For anything about which you are passionate or need to explain frequently, develop a one-minute message, a five-minute message,

and a twenty-minute message. Although you will probably use your one-minute message most often, you never know how long you will have another's attention. For example, I am often looking for opportunities to tell people about AXIS Dance Company, a nonprofit group for which I serve on the board of directors. For my one-minute message, I explain, "AXIS creates and performs high-quality contemporary dance. The pieces are developed through the collaboration of dancers with and without disabilities. AXIS teaches dance to people of all ages and educates at schools and businesses about disability and collaboration." I give them an AXIS business card with the mission statement on the back. I created these cards inexpensively on the computer. For my five-minute message, I tell them about our performances and the dancers. I describe Jacques, a former dancer who lost his foot in a car accident, and how he has reached greater heights in his work with AXIS. I tell them about Judy, Bonnie and Megan, who dance in their wheelchairs. For my twenty-minute message, I have a "Talking Points" flyer that describes the company's history, awards, and future goals.

Have I aroused your interest in AXIS Dance Company? To get started yourself, create a one-minute message describing your business or the volunteer work you do.

Maintain the self-esteem of others.

When delivering a difficult message, allow others to keep their self-esteem by using "I" phrases and giving examples. Use phrases like, "From my experience . . . " or "From Joan's book, I learned . . . " State your ideas in a collaborative spirit, such as, "I suggest we try this approach. What do you think?"

When you are giving feedback, say something positive first; no one wants to hear they could have done it better or differently. I taught my son these ideas; now he reminds me! Ask someone you trust to give you feedback on how you are doing. If you slip up or you wish you'd done something differently, be willing to say, "I'm sorry." Admitting that you made a mistake can break a pattern and allow you to move on to a productive discussion.

Maintain your self-esteem; give yourself credit.

Maintaining your own self-esteem may be the most difficult task of all. Let's examine this from a job perspective. In times of uncertainty, such as downsizing, even people with jobs are feeling fear. This can manifest itself with formerly supportive people turning inward and looking out for themselves. They may not follow the above guidelines for maintaining the self-esteem of others. This is when you must recognize your own self-worth and give yourself credit. Keeping a mini-journal is a technique that helps me. This need not take a lot of time. Although I review my life and goals extensively on an annual basis, I also keep a mini-journal consisting of brief notes made on a calendar with a square for each day. I record my highs such as, "Received kudos from VP" or "Joined a health club." I also record my lows, also known as challenges, such as, "Mom went to the hospital" or "Took a cut in salary." Recently, I was feeling overwhelmed, and my energy level was low. As I reviewed my highs and lows for the past weeks, I could see why. I could see a pattern of lows but, also, I realized how much I had accomplished. Immediately, I felt better.

Know your body; know your moods.

A journal can also be beneficial in this area. Be aware that, commonly, physical and mental well-being are closely tied. Stress can be the cause of a physical ailment, and a physical ailment can cause stress and unhappiness. If you have an extremely good day, both health-wise and mood-wise, remember what this feels like. Then when you feel a pain or a more subtle difference from the norm, take note. Do not ignore a pattern or potential problem. Catch health or mood problems early and get them treated. If you can identify why you are feeling down, it is easier to move on. Surround yourself with positive, energetic people when you are feeling down. A good listener can also help. Warning: do not let yourself get so low that you are unable to reach out for help. When you are successful at identifying and reversing a down mood, remember the technique for next time.

Take baby steps and learn as you go.

When people don't do what they are asked, the reason may be that they don't know how to get started. Break any large task into small measurable pieces. Then *do it*. Make that first phone call, give that first speech, clean the first room, and move forward. The first time I make a call to a new market, I may not know the business or terminology, so I ask a lot of questions. Then the second call goes much more smoothly. The key here is to take action. Many people have good ideas or good intentions, but the task seems overwhelming. Take that first small step, and the others will follow.

Now that I have laid the groundwork for you, I would like to finish the story about my On The Level walking tour business.

"On The Level" grew out of my childhood dream to become a physical therapist and to work with the disabled. While I had planned to pursue my goal after college, I got married, and the two did not mix. However, I never forgot my dream. I always sought volunteer work and ways of helping and working with people, even in a machine-oriented career. The dream took shape when I began planning my second career, a business to take elderly and disabled people on adventures to parks and outdoor destinations where they normally couldn't go without assistance. I thought this would happen when I retired after my son finished college. But a friend, a breast cancer survivor who knows the value of each day, encouraged me to follow my dream *now*. I revised my plan to document walks that could be done by the disabled. My son helped me as we followed our favorite paths, many where I had pushed him in a stroller when he was an infant. This meant the paths were level—no hills or steps! My son drew rough maps showing curb cuts, wheelchair-accessible rest rooms, and much more. I documented the points of interest and made notes where further research was needed. If you want to see the result, visit my Web site at OnTheLevelSF.com. (As you see, I easily slip into my *twenty-minute message* about On The Level.)

It took *many small steps* to get to a published set of self-guided walking tours. I learn every day as I *move forward* into uncharted territory. I often have so many ideas that I feel overwhelmed. First I *recognize the feeling*, the underlying stress of trying to do too much. This is when I sit down and make a list and *set priorities*. There are many *highs and lows* in pursuing my own small business, and working alone, I often have to encourage myself and *maintain my own self-esteem*.

I encourage you to pursue your dream.

# # #

For the past twenty-five years, Marilyn Straka has lived in San Francisco, where she has continued her profession as a computer consultant. An outdoors enthusiast, she has explored the neighborhoods and parks of San Francisco, both for exercise and as her hobby. Her company, On The Level, provides walking tours and publications for disabled people who want to learn more about San Francisco.

Aligning Dreams and Goals for Success

Vicki Tolman

When I was a little girl, my mom didn't allow "negative" talk about ourselves. She always told me I was very special, a gift from God, and could be anything I wanted to be when I grew up. She taught fifth grade and, on her bulletin board, she displayed the sentence, "Something good is going to happen to you." I grew up with this type of positive expectancy. I thank God for giving me a truly amazing mother who lived what she taught and taught me, from a young age, to really believe that I could do something big with my life!

I loved to dream! When I was quite young, I attended a high school football game, and it happened to be homecoming. When I saw the crown being placed on the homecoming queen's head, I started thinking that could happen to me when I grew up! I actually saw it in my mind as happening to me. Each year as my family watched the Miss America Pageant, I would walk down the middle of my family room floor from the back of the room to the front as my dad would sing, "There she is, Miss America!" In my senior year in high school, I was crowned homecoming queen of my high school. I was also a cheerleader, business editor of our yearbook, and a member of the top choir that traveled the state. When I was nineteen years old, I became Miss Tri City (the local pageant for the Miss America Pageant) representing Mesa, Tempe and Chandler, and I placed second runner-up in the Miss Arizona Pageant!

Three years ago, my husband's company announced that employees could no longer work overtime, as the company would not be able to pay for overtime work. This substantially affected our income, and I decided I needed to do something about it. Since I already worked a full-time job, I did not want another "J-O-B" where I was required to work "their schedule." That was when I decided to become a Mary Kay independent beauty consultant. I loved the products and had used them for seventeen years. I knew that a consultant could win a car in Mary Kay, and I knew that could save us more than $350 per month, as I could sell our van and eliminate both the car payment and the insurance payment.

I signed my consultant agreement in August 1999 and won the red Grand Am in November 1999! This took exactly four months! I became a Fabulous 50's Elite Independent Sales Director (a distinction shared by less than a handful of others in my state) just fifteen months after I signed my agreement.

How did I do it? Fortunately, I had a very wise senior director, Kelly, who believed in me and helped me along the way. She took a picture of my husband, Gary, and me and put it in a red Grand Am picture frame. I placed the picture on top of my microwave in the kitchen. Kelly also took a picture of me driving a red Grand Am. I placed that picture in the van I was driving. Every time I got into the van, I would think of it as my red Grand Am. I also placed that picture on my bathroom mirror and on my front door. Then I started holding classes and facials and shared the opportunity with everyone. I loved my Mary Kay business and believed with all my heart it could benefit any woman.

I set my goal with a deadline to complete Grand Am qualifications and was determined to finish before Thanksgiving. I did it!

I love to visualize and dream what can be, and I pray that God will lead me to the right women and bless my efforts. I give the Lord all the glory and praise.

As I was working towards directorship, I had a picture taken of me in the director's suit. I put this picture on my front door along with a very simple goal poster, which was a piece of paper with fifty lines that I knew I needed to fill with names of women on my team. When I started toward the director qualification, I had only nine active women in my organization and needed to have thirty within three months and a total of fifty women on my team by the fourth month. Kelly, my senior director, went to a party store and bought me a gift, which was a celebration centerpiece with the number "50" shooting up all over it in a fireworks-type arrangement. I put this by my front door, also. We completed director qualification in less than three months, before Thanksgiving 2000, and then added twenty more to our team in December. Can you imagine—December? Wow! That was Christmas, we had a family vacation planned, and I was scheduled for knee surgery that month. However, I was determined and willing to do the work. I visualized it as a done deal. When our future national sales director, Lynn Baer, came to visit at one of our meetings in early November, we all closed our eyes and pretended we had just finished the qualification. As she described the environment, the smells, and the excitement and joy of having finished this accomplishment before Thanksgiving, I saw all of this in my mind and believed it!

I have learned that, in order to accomplish something really big, it takes setting a goal with a time frame, writing it down, creating goal posters, taking pictures of you as if it has already happened, displaying those pictures in common places that you see every day, breaking the goal down into daily and weekly events, and praying that God will lead you to the right people and that His blessings will be upon you. It also requires a lot of work. One of my favorite sayings is, "Pray like everything depends upon God, and work like it all depends upon you." Positive affirmations are also a huge part of my success. On the top of my goal poster on my front door, I wrote the simple words, "Tolman's Celebration of Stars—Fabulous 50's Elite Sales Director." It was written as if I had already made it. And I did!

# # #

Vicki Tolman is a Mary Kay Fabulous 50's Elite Sales Director and has earned the use of two cars for the effective leadership of her team. A member of Phi Beta Kappa Society for top grades in college, she has held administrative positions in the Phoenix, Arizona, area.

Vicki and her husband, Gary, live in Gilbert, Arizona, and are the parents of Rochelle and Bryce.

Section IV

Focus on the Power
and
Possibilities in People!

Focus on the Power and Possibilities in People!

Joan Eleanor Gustafson

Company leaders recognize that people are their greatest assets and that they get things done through other people. They know they can't do it alone. Whether you're leading a corporation, a small business, or a community or social organization, the people around you will determine the magnitude of your success. The following recommendations will help you to become a most effective leader.

1. Surround yourself with excellent people.

Leaders have learned that one way to attract excellent people into their lives is to believe in their own excellence. Each of us is a special human being with unique skills, talents, and abilities. By truly believing in the value of her contributions, a leader will attract those people and things into her life that will ensure the success of her vision and goals.

Effective leaders know that we can control our destiny through our attitude. Therefore, it is important to remain positive, both when we are with other people and when we are alone. Positive attracts positive, and excellence attracts excellence; thus, a positive attitude will help to enlist excellent people in support of our vision.

2. Align people behind your vision and strategies.

Leaders are passionate about their vision, and they inspire a shared vision. To enlist support for their vision, leaders need to speak the language of those they wish to enlist. In order to do this, it is imperative that leaders truly care about the interests of people and understand their needs, desires, hopes, dreams, and aspirations. Ardath Rodale, CEO of Rodale, Inc., expresses this eloquently in "Lead with Your Heart," featured in this section.

In "Lessons Learned," also in this section, Dr. Debra Brittain Davenport gives an example. As a new manager, Debra subscribed to the authoritarian management style modeled by the "older and wiser" managers in her company. She shares with us her transformation into a true leader. A leader's ability to show that she cares, coupled with her enthusiasm for her vision, will inspire people to commit.

Research has shown that when leaders clearly articulate their vision for an organization, there are higher levels of commitment, motivation, loyalty, productivity, and pride in the organization. It is of utmost importance to speak positively and from the heart. In *Visionary Leadership*, Burt Nanus says, "There is no more powerful engine driving an organization toward excellence and long-range success than an attractive, worthwhile, and achievable vision of the future, widely shared."

3. Generate excitement and enthusiasm.
Excitement and enthusiasm are contagious. If a leader is truly excited about a vision or a project, others also will become excited and want to be part of it. John Hersey, leadership specialist and co-author of *The 4 Pillars of Contagious Leadership* (to be published soon), lists the following advantages for organizations when they practice what he calls "contagious leadership":

- Less attrition
- Better communications
- More effective teamwork
- Higher productivity
- Increased optimism
- Renewed creativity

- Attraction of superior talent
- Contagious leadership succession

John also discusses the advantages of contagious leadership for individuals within an organization, which include higher productivity and increased optimism, as well as more focus, fulfillment, energy, unleashed creativity, and more fun.

4. Create synergy.

Mathematics was one of my majors in college, and it took me a long time to learn that one plus one was really greater than two. Throughout my education, I had been rewarded for individual achievement. Once established in a business environment, I became aware of the power of a well-functioning team. By working with other people who may complement our strengths, we are able to enhance our results. In creating synergy, I often quote the Japanese proverb, "None of us is as smart as all of us."

5. Develop cooperative relationships and partnerships.

Although we live in a world of competition, the most effective leaders realize that the development of cooperative relationships and partnerships can contribute more to their success than focusing on competition. This earth is filled with abundance, and our relationships with others will contribute significantly to achieving our goals.

In this section, Cheryl Campbell ("Friendship and Partnerships: Building Blocks of Success") illustrates the value of networking by introducing us to some of the fascinating people she has had the pleasure of knowing.

Another aspect of the relationship/partnering equation is the value of mentoring. Later in this section, Barbara McDuffie Kahler ("Leaving a Legacy through Mentoring") tells of her experiences on both sides of the mentoring partnership. The section also includes a contribution from Dr. Kathleen Calabrese ("Inspiration + Opportunity + Courage = Personal Authority"), where she pays homage to two women who cared enough to set her on a path that she might achieve her dreams.

6. Expect the best from people.

People really do want to do their best, and they will strongly support a leader who believes in them and their abilities. Early in my career as an information systems supervisor, I had just one person reporting to me. He was a very bright computer programmer, who was new to this country and to the programming profession. Although he had not written many programs, I knew that he could accomplish anything he set out to do. Shortly after he started his job, I needed to leave town for a week. Before I left, I met with him to explain a new assignment, answer his preliminary questions, and ask him to complete a flow chart and to begin writing the programs while I was gone. When I returned, he had not only completed the things I had asked him to do, but he had also completed and run the programs successfully. I'll never forget his response when I asked him how he had done this so quickly. He said, "I know you really believed that I would be successful in this assignment. For this, I wanted to please you, so I worked late every night while you were gone so I could have it done."

If you expect the best from people, you will get the best from them. In this section, Connie Wolf ("Empowerment and Self-managing Teams") tells her story of expecting and getting the most from her people during a critical time in her company.

7. Delegate authority along with responsibility.

My husband is a diabetic and takes insulin twice each day. In order to regulate the glucose level in his blood, he uses a meter to check his blood sugar four times each day. One day, after eating breakfast, checking his glucose level, taking his insulin and reading the newspaper, he accidentally discarded his glucose meter with the newspaper. By the time he realized that his glucose meter was in the garbage can, the trash collector had already picked up the garbage. Not wanting to purchase another glucose meter, he called the manufacturer and asked the customer service representative what could be done. The representative authorized our local pharmacy to give my husband a new glucose meter at no charge, and she also committed to replace this meter for the pharmacy.

The customer service representative had the responsibility to answer customers' phone calls and also had the authority to make decisions regarding these calls. She did not have to ask a supervisor for permission. The advantages to the company are that the customer service employee knows that she is a valued employee and, as such, has a high degree of job satisfaction, and my husband is a happy customer. In this case, the company gave away an eighty-dollar item free; however, my husband is now a customer for life and will buy test strips for his meter from this company forever. These test strips cost three dollars per day.

8. Contribute to the success of others.

Linda Chandler has made an enormous difference in hundreds of thousands of people's lives, both in her leadership roles in several companies and through her seminars and keynote speeches across America and internationally. When I asked her what she considered her main purpose in life, she said, "I believe very strongly that my purpose on this planet is to help people to be all that they can be. It's to be there as a leader and to also inspire true leaders."

In this section, Laraine Rodgers ("Making Education a Priority") tells the story of earning her bachelors degree at age thirty-nine. She inspires others to do the same, no matter where they are in life.

Fulfilling the role of a mother provides one of the greatest opportunities for many women to exercise their leadership skills and to contribute to other human beings, from the time they are born to adulthood. In this section, Betty Notto ("My World—Family and Community Leadership") and Colleen Down ("The Hand that Rocks the Cradle") discuss motherhood and the fulfillment they have received from this type of leadership.

9. Recognize others for their contributions.

People love to be recognized for their achievements and accomplishments. In fact, research has shown that recognition is a greater motivator than salary. (Money can be a demotivator if there isn't enough, but it has been proven that increased salary does not necessarily create increased motivation.)

The most effective leaders do not take all the credit themselves for their achievements. Bob Woodruff once said at Coca-Cola, "There is no limit to what a man can achieve as long as he doesn't care who gets the credit." This is true also for female leaders.

When people are recognized, they are eager to support the leader in every way they can. In most cases, this means even greater contributions to the leader's goals and objectives.

10. Treat others with respect.
Effective company leaders treat their employees as they would have the employees treat their customers.

To be most successful in business, it's imperative to show utmost respect for customers. Management and employees at Marshall Field's refer to their customers as "guests." During a recent interview with a reporter, Linda Ahlers, Marshall Field's president, compared a customer to a visitor at someone's home. She said that, at your home, you would not make the visitor wait after ringing the doorbell; rather you would greet them immediately. She added that their guest relationships were not about transactions, but about relationships.

All of the leaders, who are highlighted in this book, focus on the power and the possibilities in people. This section contains contributions from strong leaders, some with more than fifty years of business experience, some who are new in business, and some who show leadership by nurturing and guiding those who will be our leaders of the future.

Lessons Learned

Debra Brittain Davenport, Ph.D.

In my younger days, the word "leadership" connoted images of Girl Scouts, high school bandleaders, and the president of the yearbook club. The concept of leadership was completely esoteric—an intangible possessed by a scant few.

Early in my corporate career, I observed "leaders" in action: yelling, back-stabbing, demeaning others, making unilateral decisions, and firing valued employees at whim. These so-called leaders were rewarded with eye-popping bonuses, coveted parking places for their luxury cars, and corner offices with their own bathrooms. Hmmm, I thought, leadership must be all about power and being in control. After all, look at the rewards for running a tight, fearful ship. This being the sum of my education in leadership, I decided these older and wiser corporate executives must know something about leadership that I did not. **Lesson #1: Choose whom you emulate very carefully.**

And so, in my very first management position, I ruled with tight-fisted authority. I was a true dictatorial maven and so proud to have my people scampering at my slightest command. Little did I know that these bright, talented, and hard-working people probably wished me dead (or at least comatose).

When one of my longtime staff members sat me down and told me a thing or two about my lack of leadership mastery, I was incredulous but, deep down, knew there was merit in his message. **Lesson #2: Accept the fact that youth and naïveté can be the most powerful of teachers.**

It was not until several years later in my career that I acquired a modicum of leadership wisdom. In 1983, I left the corporate arena to start my own business. I had observed enough organizational dysfunction and toxic management practices to know that I wanted to have a company that was founded on a new archetype—one that valued people, nurtured them, and fostered their development as human beings. This was a novel concept for 1983, but one that I was determined to bring to life. **Lesson #3: Listen to your inner voice and follow your own path.**

During the last nineteen years, I have remained committed to this principle of leadership and have refined several criteria that, in my opinion, make an exemplary leader:

1. A strong leader creates change by using *influence*, not control.
2. To be influential requires the ability to read other people and adapt to their style. Leaders are well-versed in personality, communication, and interpersonal relations, and they use this knowledge to develop and maintain rapport with others. They are outstanding *listeners*.
3. Leaders happily put others first. *Always.*
4. Leaders take feelings into account. They have a heart and aren't the least bit afraid to show it.
5. Leaders live authentically, without pretense or affectation.
6. Leaders have a lively sense of humor and use it frequently.
7. Leaders have highly developed insight, intuition, and flexibility. They spend time developing acuity in left and right-brain function.
8. Leaders provide encouragement and validation. (You would be amazed how many people have never received encouragement from their parents when they were growing up.)

9. A strong leader can undo damage that has been done by others.

10. Leaders are *mentors*, not managers.

11. Leaders are never complacent. They are always thirsty for knowledge and are committed to lifelong learning. They share their knowledge freely with others and encourage others' personal and professional development.

12. Leaders have a passion for directing the spotlight on others. They get a real kick out of stepping into the background while someone else shines.

13. Leaders live their lives from the perspective of abundance. They know there is plenty to go around, so they are generous with their time, knowledge, and resources.

Interestingly, many people believe they are not—or never could be—leaders when, in fact, we are all leaders whether at home, on the job, in school, or at play with our children. Our behavior, and that means *everything* we do, sets the standard for those around us. Personal leadership, the concept of leading oneself, is the foundation of leadership for all of us. As my friend, Dr. Ray Russell says, "You can't lead others if you can't lead yourself." How true!

In essence, true leaders are self-actualized people who possess the wisdom, confidence, self-discipline, and emotional intelligence that enables them to focus on others, rather than their own self-interest. Granted, focusing on others rather than yourself is not easy to reach and maintain; it is human nature to feel fear, anxiety, and the "what ifs" that cause us to reserve our good work only for ourselves. However, if we allow this to happen, we cease being the leader that others can turn to for guidance, support, and motivation. **Lesson #4: Keep giving, even in the face of fear and scarcity.** Your rewards will be many and great.

Richard Moss said, "The greatest gift you can give another is the purity of your attention." Give your full attention to someone today. Listen with an open mind, and offer anything you can to support them. *This is leadership.*

# # #

Debra Brittain Davenport, Ph.D., is the CEO of DavenportFolio, a licensed firm supporting professional individuals with career development and Certified Professional Mentoring™. DavenportFolio is headquartered in Scottsdale, Arizona, and serves clients both nationally and internationally.

Lead with Your Heart

Ardath H. Rodale

From the time I was a small child, people have commented that my eyes looked as if they were way ahead of me. I feel as if I have had many lives, but, in looking back, they all seem to have built to where I am today. I must have had a guardian angel. I have faced many hard times. Through the years as I faced these challenges, I didn't ask, "Why me?" but rather asked, "What can I learn from this experience?"

When I married Robert Rodale, I told myself that, in marrying him, I had also married the mission of the family and the company of Rodale Press. At that time, the mission was to help people take more control of their lives by eating food that was grown without chemicals and pesticides so that they could be healthier.

It was Bob's idea that he would take care of the company, and I would take care of the family. However, I needed more creative challenges for the growth of my spirit. I was twenty-six years old when I began my work as a volunteer for the company. My mission expanded to make the working environment for all employees the best that it could be. I used cheerful colors for the walls and the family's art collection to adorn the offices. Why shouldn't a person's office space look as if it were their home away from home? We all knew each other in the company and were on a first name basis. We worked together; we were friends.

When I realized that I was spending more of my day at the office than at home, I told Bob I wished to be paid. His reply was, "But, I don't want a wife who works." I won!

I was appointed director of environmental resources, responsible for all details regarding corporate buildings and office space. Since Rodale always has been a proponent of environmental health, one of my duties was to recycle and renovate older buildings in the community to be used for more office space as the company grew.

Since few women of my generation worked outside the home, I was continually frustrated by my female friends who had no conception of the extent of my work. They constantly asked me, "What *do* you do?" My answer to myself was, "I just reach out and do what's in my heart."

After my son, David, died in 1985 from AIDS, I began writing my first book, *Climbing Toward the Light*. I found writing the chapter on my mother was particularly difficult for me. Knowing I was struggling, Bob asked to read it one morning at breakfast. He said, "No, Ardie, this is all wrong. You must get into your mother's head and try to visualize what she is feeling." As I rewrote the chapter, I realized he was 100 percent right. I have never forgotten this in my writing or in my duties as head of the company. I need to constantly put myself in the other person's place, a vantage point, which has reinforced my need to express deeper compassion and understanding for all people.

In 1990, Bob was killed in an automobile accident in Russia, and I became chairman and CEO of Rodale. At that time, the company's chief operating officer, a longtime employee and friend, taught me the second important lesson. He told me not to make any important decisions during the first month. Instead, he advised me to go *into* the offices of the other executives to *hear* what they were thinking and to listen to their vision and what they felt was important as the company moved forward.

As a way of communicating with employees and some friends, I began writing motivational messages—always on brightly colored paper—as a way to catch their eye and invite feedback from them.

When the time came to search for a new chief operating officer for the company, many employees were fearful of the changes that might take place. I challenged the employees to put their best foot forward, to move ahead, and to *work together* with possibility thinking. Everyone in the company needed to be aligned, and I listed the power points for success:

- *Imagine* that you *are* a winner, and *believe* it!
- *Be* a trendsetter—a leader, not a follower.
- *Listen* to what other people are saying and feeling.
- *Care* about each other and *reach* out willingly to help.
- *Respect* each other's differences in life style and opinions.
- *Communicate* openly and honestly.
- *"Thank you"* is one of the most important courtesies in life.
- *Bringing* others along with you is more productive than stepping on others.
- *Remember* to laugh and have fun and to enjoy all the free gifts of nature and the treasures of our families.
- Happiness is an inside job!

My greatest aspiration as a female entrepreneur and leader of our company is to stand as a positive force for educating people everywhere in the process of helping the world build healthy soil to grow healthy food to feed healthier people.

Our purpose is to inspire and enable people to improve their lives and the world around them.

Our company values are:

- The Power to Heal
- The Responsibility to Listen
- The Passion to Innovate
- The Virtue of Teamwork
- The Value of Growth

It is exciting to see that we are expanding internationally, and we have made many very special friends through reaching out. We want all our employees to feel connected to our mission and to work as a team to accomplish it.

Now, more than ever, we need world leaders who lift our spirits and encourage us to work for communities, world peace, and love. Each individual needs to know that they are a special child of God and are loved unconditionally. As we individuals strive to be healthy, it is imperative that we work at the same time for a safer, healthier world where we can each offer the best of what is in our minds, bodies, and spirits.

I often search to find the meaning in life and continually ask myself, "Why am I here?" All of us travel many paths, searching for ways to turn dreams into reality. Most often, we look outside ourselves.

All actions, thoughts, and achievements stem from the quiet center of who you are; that place of peace, energy, and love. Once you find that precious center, you carry it with you wherever you go.

# # #

Ardath Harter Rodale is chairman of the board of Rodale Inc. and chairman emeritus of the board of the Rodale Institute. She is the author of three books: *Climbing Toward the Light*, *Gifts of the Spirit*, and *Reflections: Finding Love, Hope, and Joy in Everyday Life*. She has received two honorary doctor of humane letters: One from Allentown College of Saint Francis de Sales in Allentown, Pennsylvania, and the other from Lehigh University in Bethlehem, Pennsylvania, and an honorary doctor of laws degree from Kutztown University. She is the mother of five and grandmother of ten.

Friendships and Partnerships: Building Blocks of Success

Cheryl Campbell

I'd like to tell you how I survived thirty years in a predominantly male industry and lived to be successful. As the daughter of a southern belle, wife of an attorney, and mother of two boys, I have also enjoyed a fabulous thirty-year career in telecommunications and technology. My career began in an era of Vietnam and protest, and it continues now in my most current role as vice president, public relations, for a global outsourcing and technology company. I thought it important to emphasize where I came from, and where I am now, before I tell you how I accomplished some of my greatest successes as a female leader in a predominantly male business world.

I tell my friends (friends are key in the story) that I feel like Forrest Gump, because I was always in the right place at the right time as new opportunities opened for women. Many opportunities opened for me when I became the first female elected as both officer and vice president at Cincinnati Bell, Inc. I later had the exciting privilege of leading the communications efforts to take Cincinnati Bell's spin-off company, Convergys, public. My job has taken me from dinner in the boardroom of the New York Stock Exchange to lunch at the Forbes Town House (and a private tour of the artwork of the Faberge Collection) to a private dinner at Kensington Palace. Pretty heady stuff for a history major from South Bend, Indiana!

But this story is not about me. It's about the relationships that have helped me hold onto myself in an era when I was a "Mrs." in a "Ms." world and when I chose to ride the feminist wave in pearls and Pappagallos. I've learned how to accept and capitalize on my differences from male counterparts in the corporate world and have also survived challenging times in my personal life. I'm proud of the commitments I've made to community organizations. My firm conviction is that it's always about relationships.

Reflecting over a fantastic career, the experiences that really matter are those that have led me to treasure the value of friendships. The greatest influence on my life has been from some very special women. Some have been friends who inspired me to participate in philanthropic and business endeavors. Others have been business partners, who became sounding boards and endless sources of wisdom and compassion in dealing with everyday challenges in my personal and professional life.

Donna West has had a tremendous influence over my philanthropic achievements. She was the first friend I made in Cincinnati when I moved here thirty years ago and, together, we filled many hours with community volunteerism. Inspired by the care that she received from Hospice during the last days of her life, I made a commitment to the Hospice board in support of my dear friend, Donna, and her husband, with whom I have the privilege of serving on the board. This is one of my most cherished achievements. Because of Donna, I'm passionately involved with any organization that gives comfort and dignity to a person's final time on earth. Even though Donna passed away eleven years ago, she is still influencing my life and the decisions I make regarding community service.

While working at Cincinnati Bell and responsible for its charitable foundation, I chose to take a chance and sponsor a new nonprofit organization dedicated to educating women about health issues. Dianne Dunkelman, founder and president of Speaking of Women's Health, and I worked closely to outline details of our sponsorship. As this venture grew from a one-day, annual event in Cincinnati to events in thirty-two cities nationwide, our friendship flourished. Supporting this first-class event was much more rewarding than I had ever imagined. Thousands of women have been educated over the past five years on important health issues. The hundreds of stories that come from the women who go to the seminars are overwhelming. Some have learned and have committed themselves to doing breast self-exams leading to early breast cancer detection and survival. Others have taken advantage of free bone-density scans at the conferences and have detected early signs of osteoporosis in time to stop the disease from progressing. Dianne, who possesses an equal combination of beauty, wit, and grit, and I continue to work together on other community events while enjoying social activities that include our families. When my oldest son became ill with depression, she was such an inspiration. Her willingness to open up and share her own personal experiences helped me tremendously.

At a Cincinnati Opera brunch a few years ago, I stood in the buffet line loading my plate with a glob of chicken casserole and turned to see this gorgeous, trim, sophisticated woman who greeted me with a warm smile and big hello. I'm sure she looks better rolling out of bed in the morning than I do after a trip to the spa! Her name is Melody Sawyer Richardson. Over brunch we had a casual conversation, which produced exciting plans regarding partnerships in the arts community. Melody's educational, professional, and community leadership achievements are lengthy enough to make most people a bit envious, but one can't help but love her. Planning community projects with Melody gives me a sense of joy. Surprise notes she sends me at the office on beautiful cards give me a boost when I need it most and expect it least. Most recently she said in a note, "When I grow up I want to be just like you." One can't help but have a great day after getting a note like that. I don't think there's anything Melody can't do, and I want to be just like *her* when *I* grow up!

A huge laugh with a friend now and then helps me keep my sanity. It's the energizer I need to move on to another career project or assignment that may be overwhelming. Friends and laughter keep us alive. If we don't have a great time, we're not going to have the energy, patience, or kindness needed to succeed at anything. My dear friend Carrie Van Derzee's intuition, as well as her playfulness, kicks in on the days I'm too serious. She phones me with an anecdote or old story of our past escapades. Suddenly I'm laughing so hard, I'm crying and my stomach aches. The deadlines and brimming lists of projects suddenly aren't so overwhelming. She's outrageous and helps me keep my perspective. Together, we're truly "Lucy and Ethel."

Through the years, it has been these relationships, this strong network of kind, compassionate women who mean the world to me, that has given me the insight and courage to forge ahead in both my career and my personal life.

I have talked mostly about what I have received, but I think it's important to mention that, over the years, I have not forgotten how to give to many business and personal relationships. I encourage everyone to consider creative, fun, and uplifting ways to reach out to people who are important in their lives.

To accomplish the things you consider really important in life, you need to begin with a solid foundation of friendships and relationships. A case in point is that, after he wrote his first fund-raising request to potential donors, George W. Bush knew he had a shot at raising the money and getting the support to mount a campaign. And, the source? He drew on the years of long-term friendships and relationships from his mother's Christmas card list!

Nurturing your personal and business relationships will not only enhance your life, but will also contribute to making you a strong leader.

# # #

Cheryl N. Campbell is vice president, public relations and corporate communications, for Convergys Corporation, the global leader in providing billing services and customer and employee care services that transform customer relationships into a competitive advantage.

In her role as chief communications officer, Cheryl has primary responsibility for corporate reputation, executive and financial communications, media relations, internal communications, corporate philanthropy, and government relations.

Cheryl graduated from Purdue University and studied at Dartmouth University and University of Pennsylvania's Wharton School of Business.

The Hand that Rocks the Cradle

Colleen Down

Over the years I have had a scientific exploritorium on the window-sill above my kitchen sink. I have watched as the tadpoles that my boys caught in the irrigation ditch behind our house lost their tails, sprouted legs, and turned into full-fledged frogs. I have watched as lima beans planted on a wet paper towel in a Ziploc bag broke through their hard outer shell, sent down roots, and then sent up sprouts. I have lingered long over my dishes to watch as tiny green caterpillars, ordered from a mail order catalogue, spun cocoons, hung for weeks from the lids of the jars, and emerged as beautiful monarch butterflies. I am still thrilled by the wonder of Mother Nature. Perhaps it's because I, too, am a mother. From my vantage point in front of my kitchen sink, I have also watched as babies, playing at my feet, have transformed before my eyes from toddlers, through the awkwardness of junior high years, and then to become radiant brides. I have watched my boys transform from Mutant Ninja Turtles to Power Rangers to good, strong men. Mother Nature and I have a lot in common. We know that inside every green caterpillar is a beautiful butterfly and inside every pink, squirming, naked baby is endless and eternal potential.

A mother is the ultimate visionary. Within a mother's heart is held the hope of all that a child can become. Even before that baby is cradled in her arms, a mother begins to dream and plan and prepare. She dreams of the day the baby will arrive. Then, when that newborn child is laid in her arms, in a fleeting moment, she pictures those first steps, the first day of school, proms, graduations, a wedding, and grandchildren. A mother sees a lifetime of hope and promise. Then the epidural begins to wear off, the relatives go home, the husband rolls over and goes to sleep, and the mother is left with her dreams and a very large pile of laundry.

From this point on, our dreams are kept in a tiny corner of our hearts, and the day-to-day realities of life settle upon us. There are meals to prepare, Band-Aids to be applied, and spilled milk to be wiped up. There are times when the only vision we have for our children is the vision of a child who can use the toilet independently. The school years come upon us and we carpool, school shop, anguish over the multiplication tables, and attend a lot of soccer games (even though very few of us ever picture our children becoming professional soccer players). Soon we find ourselves becoming drivers ed teachers, helping correct research papers at 2:00 A.M., and trying to once again remember what our child looked like before he dyed his hair. Somehow, through the years, because we know that every tadpole grows legs and every caterpillar grows wings, we keep the vision and show our children the way.

We remind our children after every lost tryout or failed audition that they still have talent, that they are worthwhile, and that there will be a next time. We remind them after every lost love and broken heart that things will work out. We encourage them through junior high. We keep their college dreams alive when they just cannot grasp their chemistry class. We remind our girls that they are princesses and comment on our boy's growing stature. We are the dream keepers. We are the visionaries. We are the coaches and the cheerleaders and the huggers when they cross the finish line. And we do it not for the masses but for one child at a time.

Perhaps the greatest elements of true leadership are to remind others of their potential, give hope for the future, and then to show the way by precept and example. We live in a time when the way is often unclear and there is a great need for leaders to stand strong and to be a light. Leaders need to have a clear vision and to exemplify those ideals that they espouse. There is no greater place to do this than within the walls of our own homes. The great anthropologist Margaret Mead said, "Never doubt that a small group of dedicated individuals can change the world; indeed, it is the only thing that ever has." Is there anyone more dedicated to a cause, more dedicated to a person, more dedicated to a vision than a mother is to a child?

Abraham Lincoln said, "All that I am and all that I ever hope to be I owe to my angel mother." He was actually speaking of his stepmother, Sarah Johnson. Sarah saw in the awkward, eleven-year-old Abe something special. From the first day that she came into the Lincoln home, she took him under her wing. She taught him to read and do math, and she never let him forget the potential that he had to become someone great. He never once felt like she loved him any less than her own three children. Likewise, Lincoln's great counterpart, George Washington, also said, "My mother was the most beautiful woman I ever saw. All I am I owe to my mother. I attribute all my success in life to the moral, intellectual, and physical education I received from her." In these and in so many, many other cases, it has been the unknown vision and unseen hand of a mother, rocking a cradle, which has helped to shape the world.

So much of a mother's work often seems mundane and ordinary, and we may often find ourselves asking, "Is this worth it?" However, we can never forget the light we are to the rising generation. Out of small means, cometh great things. As I watch the row of seeds growing in the tray behind my kitchen sink, reaching upwards towards the sunlight, I remind myself that my hands, immersed in dishwater, have the power to change the world.

# # #

Colleen Down is author of the book, *It Takes a Mother to Raise a Village*. Although she holds a degree in home economics education, all of her training has been on the front lines of family life. Colleen and her husband, Steve, are the parents of seven children ranging from preschool to college. Colleen considers herself an advocate and cheerleader for mothers everywhere.

Making Education a Priority

Laraine Rodgers

From my earliest years, I was told that I would be successful. My nuclear family's messages regularly inspired, challenged, and drove me to achieve. Whether it was my maternal grandmother (a stay-at-home mother of ten children) who repeated that, "Laraine would never starve," or my mom (a college graduate who was born in 1905 and had an uninterrupted career in social work and management) telling me to do my best, or any of a number of relatives who coached and coaxed me onward, the directives were clear. Just as important, they led by example.

Yet for all I had accomplished through grit and determination, finishing college somehow eluded me. I had married early and had two wonderful children and an exciting career in information technology. I juggled work and home, trying from time to time to take college classes, and actually accrued some college credit, but when priorities were set, school never made it to the top three. My excuse was that I had much training at work in technology and management . . . and I wasn't starving! New hires, however, all seemed to have degrees as well as experience.

In the summer of 1985, I was selected to attend a one-week Business of Banking (BOB) School at the University of Colorado in Boulder. There were 100 of us in the program, in twenty groups of five persons each. We were to simulate running a bank, with various metrics set to determine who ran the best banking entity. Class demographics showed that more than 90 percent of the attendees had college degrees, and more than 30 percent had one or more graduate degrees. After day one, I realized that I was just as knowledgeable as most of the multi-degreed students; yet I was categorized as much less educated. I vowed that I would complete my B.S. degree before I turned forty. When I returned home, I enrolled in a thirteen-month college completion program from the University of San Francisco. Completing the program was a struggle—I had to contend with much business travel, two unexpected surgeries, and the general complexities of life, but I persevered and graduated at age thirty-nine years and eleven months. Now that I was in the habit of studying and writing, I went on to earn my MBA at Pepperdine University and completed this two years later!

The degrees made a difference, in many ways. Yes, the career opportunities did increase, and the business theory I learned made doing my jobs easier. I met great people, both faculty and students, who enriched my life. Many of these people are still friends. I learned much more than theory—in particular, I learned that I, too, must set the example, just as my parents and grandparents had done for me. Several of my co-workers, including my assistant and one of the vice presidents in my organization, went back to school and earned their degrees.

I make it a personal priority to encourage, coach, and coax my colleagues, staff, and friends (as well as my own children) to continue their education (as learning is a lifelong endeavor). We must set the example—communicating what is important and living our words.

# # #

Laraine Rodgers is president and executive director of the Arizona Partnership for Higher Education and Business. Her experience spans leadership positions in industry and government. Laraine is the chairwoman of the Tri-University (Arizona State University, Northern

Arizona University, and University of Arizona) Master of Engineering Program's Industry Advisory Board. She was an adjunct faculty member at Arizona State University School of Business from 1995 to 1998, teaching information technology, entrepreneurship, and strategy.

Leaving a Legacy through Mentoring

Barbara McDuffie Kahler

An exceptional leader focuses not only on vision and execution but also on the people and the power that evolves when people are challenged and supported to be their very best. Coaching and mentoring are competencies that every successful leader uses to inspire and develop others—thereby, leaving a legacy for the future.

Many successful leaders have demonstrated this characteristic in my life. My first vivid memory of inspiring and developing others came during my own high school years. My guidance counselor, John Metcalf, challenged me to focus on my passion and being the best I could possibly be. Mr. Metcalf also suggested that I go to college, and he supported me in locating work/study and loan programs that would assist me. He inspired me to study hard. As a result, I finished in first place in my graduating class and was the first in my family to attend college. When I was growing up in a small, rural Missouri town, I could never have imagined that one day I would have a successful career as a corporate executive!

For a leader, the benefits of being a mentor are significant. The mentor's primary purpose is to develop the knowledge, skills, and experience critical to an organization's growth and competitive advantage. Individuals are inspired for career growth. The leader gains from both the business success and from the satisfaction of aiding the development of another human being.

Although many leaders possess the natural ability to guide individuals through the mentoring process, a key skill is teaching others to integrate mentoring skills with their other leadership competencies. Here is a simple six-step process that has been effective for me:

1. **Prepare**—assess readiness for mentoring, barriers to success, and goals for the mentoring relationship.
2. **Identify** possible mentors—make a list.
3. **Recruit** your mentor—call for an appointment. Discuss goals and commitment.
4. **Define** the relationship—set protocols and expectations.
5. **Manage** the relationship—prepare for meetings, communicate openly, and record progress.
6. **Evaluate** the relationship—schedule periodic reviews and evaluations.

The opportunities to be mentored and coached came to me many times in my corporate career. Another memorable milestone was when I made a major career change from being an administrative manager to becoming a systems engineer in a sales position. This change led to many future job opportunities and a successful sales and marketing career. The results have been overwhelming, leading to an early retirement from my corporate career and starting my own business. I guess one could say that coaching and mentoring "got in my blood." I have a strong passion to develop others. Moving beyond the corporate world, I now volunteer for two organized mentoring programs—Big Brothers/Big Sisters and City of Tempe, Women in Business.

It is rewarding to be a mentor, as well as to be the one who is mentored. Coaching and mentoring not only help to build better leaders, but they also leave a legacy for the future.

# # #

Barbara McDuffie Kahler is an executive coach with a proven track record for developing people and delivering results. She relies on more than thirty years of corporate executive and leadership experience at IBM to coach technical and executive women and their organizations to achieve their greatness in business, career, and life balance. She guides clients to establish a vision, set goals, develop an action plan, and focus on achieving winning results.

At IBM, she coached hundreds individually and in groups as she led new business start-ups and built high-performance teams. She created the women's leadership institutes that contributed to a 200 percent increase in the number of female executives at IBM. The strategic alliances she negotiated with software developers tripled the sources of software applications for the company's server products.

My World—Family and Community Leadership

Betty Notto

My stories of leadership may be very unlike the other women featured in this book. I believe that I am more mentor than leader.

After my youngest son, Randy, finished college, married and left the family nest, I ventured briefly into the business world. Because my husband, Len, and I enjoyed collecting wildlife art prints, we opened an art gallery. Len thought that I would be lonely and bored after forty years of having children living in our home. (In reality, I was rejoicing and enjoying the peace and quiet.)

I disliked going to work from 10:00 A.M. until 6:00 P.M. each day, because it cramped my style. It seemed I had no time for myself, and I didn't have the energy for the volunteer activities that I enjoyed.

After two years and a $50,000 loss, we closed the art gallery. We discovered that other people didn't enjoy collecting wildlife art as much as we did.

In all honesty, I can say that I have never missed being a part of the business world. I have had and still do have a career. I'm a wife, mother, grandmother, great-grandmother, sister, sister-in-law, mother-in-law, aunt, friend, and volunteer. My career has been filled with many rewards, such as being there when a child takes his first steps and learns to say "da da" and "ma ma," being the first person to see a child's report card, knowing how hard he or she worked to earn good grades in school, and helping a son or daughter get dressed on prom night.

There were many quiet tears shed as each of my children boarded the school bus on the first day of kindergarten, as we left them at their college dormitory, and as I witnessed their marriage vows when they found "the right person."

Letting go has always been difficult for me. I prayed for divine guidance, and God answered, "It's time—let go."

The children are adults now, but there are sixteen grandchildren and eleven great-grandchildren. I've become one of those grandmas who spoils them. The hugs, sloppy kisses, and "I love yous" make my life complete.

I enjoy my career, that of being me, a little old lady with extra pounds on the hips and thighs, who loves people and has had the same man hold her hand for fifty-seven years.

If I had spent years working outside my home, I probably would have more money and worldly possessions today, but money could not buy the fulfilling life I've lived and am living today. When I look at my children today, I can say to myself, "Job well done, Lizzy." Both my husband and I have truly enjoyed parenting our six children.

One day in the mid-1960s, while walking through the upstairs hall in our home, I noticed an empty bedroom. "This can't be," I thought as I entered the room. The Notto family home was always filled to the brim with people, both large and small. In a fifteen-month time span, our only daughter and oldest son married, and my invalid mother, who lived with us part-time, passed away.

Len and I decided to look into adopting a baby girl (to fill that empty room and the empty spot in our hearts). At an informational meeting at an adoption agency, we learned that most couples want to adopt a baby, and older children were more difficult to place. We then decided to adopt an older child, because we had already experienced the joy that a new baby brings into a family. After giving birth to a daughter and then four sons, I really wanted another girl who would like frilly dresses, curly hair and Barbie dolls.

Three months later, we met our seven-year-old daughter, Carla, and soon learned that she wasn't into the dolls and the dollhouse furniture I had collected for her. She was a shy child who captured our hearts at our first meeting when she wrapped one little arm around Len's neck and the other around my neck and asked us, "Will you be my 'real' mommy and daddy?" She had lived in a foster home where there were "real" kids and foster kids. The "real" kids had more privileges than the foster kids, and she wanted to become a "real" kid. As for the dolls, we donated them to the Goodwill Industries, because Carla didn't use them. Instead, she followed her dad around as he did repairs on our home and lake cabin. She became dad's helper, as she learned how to handle a saw, hammer, and screwdriver. Carla and her dad share a special bond today and always will.

It didn't take very long for Carla to become our "real" kid— real and loved. We like to tell her that she is special to us because she's our only chosen child. Our special daughter is forty-two years old now and works with learning-disabled children. She has four of the world's most beautiful children, one husband, one dog, and one cat. We are so proud of the beautiful, caring, and compassionate woman she has become. She is one of my success stories, and there are five other accomplished children in our family.

This past week, I had my youngest great-grandchild, Erika, keeping me company while her mother trained for employment. Great-grandpa and I enjoyed having her. It took the two of us to care for this thirteen-pound baby, and figuring out how to get her into and out of her car seat was mind-boggling. We now know why God sends babies to young, energetic people and not to old fogies. We love you, Erika—you are our newest miracle.

I believe that every mother has a leadership role. Guiding, encouraging, affirming, and mentoring her children can be the most important thing she accomplishes in her lifetime. Being a mother has been a joy for me. I don't wish to brag (well, perhaps I do a wee bit), but my six kids truly are the most intelligent and successful people on the face of the earth. Oh, and did I mention beautiful, too?

While my children were growing up, I decided to engage in some volunteer work. Because of my volunteer activities, I've met and befriended people not only from the United States, but from other countries as well. Some of the relationships formed have become priceless, and I have extended my family in this way.

In 1978, while attending a conference at Marquette University in Wisconsin, we met Father Michael O'Donohue from Dublin, Ireland, and we invited him to spend some time with our family before returning to Ireland. That was the beginning of a close friendship with Michael. He visited us ten times, and we were able to visit him in Ireland. During these visits, we gained a new understanding of the Irish and the ongoing battle in Northern Ireland, and he learned about life in America. Before each visit, Michael would call to tell me that he was craving American ice cream so I would stock the freezer for him. Our dear friend died last year. We miss him and the friendship we shared. Michael would always call us on two American holidays, Independence Day and Thanksgiving. When the phone rang as we were having Thanksgiving dinner, someone would always say, "It's Father Michael calling to share Thanksgiving with us, and I bet the Irish have never seen a Pilgrim or a Native-American."

At our first meeting, Michael told us that we Americans are too demonstrative because we go around hugging others. After one week at our home, he became a hugger, too. It was obvious that he enjoyed the hugs, and I think that he visited us whenever he was lonely and needed lots of hugs.

When our son, Dan, and his wife, Pam, moved from Minnesota to New York City a few years ago, they left a car with us and instructed us to give it to a needy family. Through the refugee committee at church, we met Zijad and Jasminka and their family. They were refugees from the war in Bosnia and had just arrived in Minnesota to start a new life in America. They did not own a car. Their family consists of two daughters, one son, and two grandchildren. We bonded with this family at our first meeting. They had been through the horrors of war and lost everything they owned. Their stories of the terrible things that happened to them still bring tears to my eyes. We mentored this family and have become close friends. My husband hired Zijad to work in our family business. Jasminka and the two daughters have found employment, also. In two years, they saved enough money for a down payment on a home of their own in a suburb of St. Paul. Very kind and loving people, they are constantly doing things for us, such as cleaning the snow off our driveway in winter and raking our lawn in spring. They have become "family" to us. We love them dearly, are very proud of them, and thank God for sending them to us.

When Len and I had been married for twenty-eight years, some friends suggested that we join them for a marriage enrichment weekend called "Marriage Encounter." That weekend we experienced a deeper love for each other than we had ever known before. Through the busy years of raising the children and developing the business, we didn't have time and energy for the two of us. At the end of the Marriage Encounter, we renewed our marriage vows, our commitment to each other. We felt a closeness that we had never experienced in the past. I wanted to get active and share what we found on that weekend with other couples, but Len was reluctant, because he is a shy person. He didn't think that he could share stories of his life with strangers. When the group leader gently prodded him to try it, we did. That was twenty-nine years ago, and we are still leading other couples to the ultimate joys of marriage and parenthood.

Through Marriage Encounter, we have developed the confidence to give reflections on marriage in churches at Sunday services. It is so great to meet couples who believe in married love, and this strengthens our love and commitment to each other. Through the years, my introvert husband has become an extrovert!

For the past few years, each time we lead a Marriage Encounter weekend, Len says, "This is our last weekend as lead-couple. We are too old. Other couples can't relate to us." I say, "Okay," knowing in my heart that there will always be another weekend with us as leaders. But on each weekend that we are facilitators, couples tell us that we helped them learn to communicate like never before.

At the end of the last Marriage Encounter when we served on the team, several couples wrote on the weekend evaluations that we touched their hearts and they want to be together as long as we have been together. One couple wrote that they want to be like us when they grow up. One man put a note under our door. It read: "Thank you, thank you, thank you!! You have helped me to appreciate the beautiful girl I married in 1968."

Marriage Encounter has given me the opportunity to share a ministry with my husband. We grow closer to each other each time we volunteer to be team leaders on a weekend. The younger couples we mentor and train to be weekend facilitators call us "Mom and Dad," and we have tons of honorary grandchildren. We love it!

Several years ago, the pastoral minister at my church told me that she thought that I was a leader/mentor. She asked me to attend classes at the seminary and become a coordinator of the BeFriender ministry at our parish. BeFriender ministry educates and supports women and men as leaders for a listening ministry of care. BeFrienders visit with people who are hurting emotionally, the sick, the lonely, and the depressed. They visit anyone who needs a listening friend to help them through a tough time. For the past fifteen years, I have been training, mentoring, and leading others in this ministry. At my church we have eighteen women and four men in the BeFriender program, and I enjoy conducting the training for the listening workshop. Since most of us would rather speak than listen, many people are not good listeners. By the last training session, the newly trained BeFrienders know the difference between hearing and listening. I feel a sense of accomplishment when the new

BeFriender ministers are commissioned at a Sunday service. It's almost like giving birth (but not as painful!)

Each Thursday at 10:00 A.M., as a BeFriender, I visit a beautiful eighty-nine-year-old homebound widow who had a stroke. She has difficulty speaking and hearing—but in spite of that, we two seniors have a great gabfest.

Even in various areas of volunteerism, women are leaders.

God has richly blessed me through the years with a busy and happy life. I wouldn't trade places with any other woman. I like being me!

# # #

In addition to her leadership role as a mother, grandmother and great-grandmother, Betty Notto volunteers more than 1,000 hours of her time each year to nonprofit organizations. She fulfills leadership responsibilities within her church women's organization, BeFrienders, Marriage Encounter, and several other organizations. Betty and her husband, Len, also provide training and mentoring to engaged couples. She has been quoted in several magazines and newspapers.

Betty and Len have been married for fifty-seven years and have received the WCCO radio station "Good Neighbor" recognition.

Inspiration + Opportunity + Courage = Personal Authority

Kathleen Calabrese, Ph.D.

A leader is a person who chooses to actively and compassionately cultivate the attributes and behaviors in another, which will enable that person at the time of death to say. "I have lived my truth. I have been the author of my life, and for that, I am deeply grateful."

Interestingly, this definition of leadership came easily to me, so I knew that it lived within me. I knew it resonated with my life and was a part of my story, so I allowed it to be my springboard for this piece. I hope it will lead you to your own beloved, familiar territory.

As I contemplated the question, "Am I a leader?" and I heard myself say, "Yes. Yes, I am a leader," I was brought back to the early years of my story where the seeds of leadership were sown and nurtured by two women who saw something powerful and important in me and made it their business to help me begin to see it too. They were leaders. They helped me begin to author my life.

My seventh-grade English teacher, Mrs. Bersuck, and my principal, Miss Dunay, saw potential in me, but they also saw that paralyzing fear and anxiety eclipsed this potential. I'm not sure how much they knew about my father's alcoholism—no one talked in those days—but they did see my suffering and my struggle. They saw a bright child whose written words could not be read aloud, because the hand that held the paper shook so violently, and the throat that held the voice was clogged with self-consciousness and shame.

I wish I could go back and surreptitiously listen to the details and nuance of their conversation—the one where they concocted an antidote for a frightened child, but this is what I do know came from that conversation. I agreed to participate in the Richmond Speaking Contest, an annual event designed to provide Buffalo Public School children an opportunity to hone their public speaking skills by memorizing a piece of their choice and delivering it in the most dramatic, effective and heartfelt way possible to an audience and panel of judges.

I am still overwhelmed when I think of the courage that I was able to muster in order to say yes to the challenge offered me by those two ordinary women who provided extraordinary leadership to me at a critical time in my life.

Miss Dunay spent hours with me. I can still see her standing in the rear of the gymnasium/auditorium after school, prompting me to articulate, project, inspire, and "slooow downnnnnnn." Each evening, poised in front of my bedroom mirror, I spoke the words over and over and over again.

The day of the speaking contest, my hands still shook, but not as much, and my voice was strong and clear. The piece I chose—I have forgotten its title—tugged at the heartstrings, and I thought that the reason I won was because it provoked tears. When I won the regional contest with a stirring rendition of the poem, "The Highwayman," I began to think of myself in a slightly different way. I was not as afraid.

Finally the day came to compete for the title of citywide champion of the Richmond Speaking Contest. Midway through the poem, my mind stopped working, and the words stopped flowing. I stood, seeking composure through the fear and confusion, and I found it, much to every audience member's relief. My voice rode with the words to the poem's conclusion, and I was met with warm applause.

I came in second that day. The winner became my best friend in high school. The seeds of leadership and personal authority, so carefully planted in me by two caring women, took root that day. I learned I could survive humiliation, and I could conquer fear. I learned I did not need to be perfect. I only needed to stay with myself and finish.

Today, I am a psychotherapist, and yes, I am a leader. For eighteen years, I have sat with my clients, listening to their stories, bearing witness to their pain and their triumphs, and helping them take tentative steps and bold leaps to their inner truth and knowing.

I listen with my heart, and I take my cues from the courageous people who entrust me with their most tender and vulnerable selves. I ask questions couched in compassion. I attend to them, to changes I see coming over their faces as we enter into deep conversation, to the way their bodies move in response to the words that hang in the air, and I direct them to "go deeper."

The stories of our lives hold the key to our own greatness. As a leader, I honor the story and ask for more and more detail. As a leader, I challenge my clients to make choices that reflect a commitment to their own hero's journey, rather than acquiescing to fear or the pleading of others to "mend my life," as Mary Oliver describes so powerfully in her poem, "The Journey."

Yes, many people beyond Mrs. Bersuck and Miss Dunay helped me to claim my own authority, to hone my leadership skills. After all, life is a never-ending process of learning, and learning and learning again to have faith in oneself. I am grateful to everyone, known and unknown to me, who has pushed, prodded, and walked with me. I gladly take up their mantle to lead, armed with my own personal authority.

# # #

Kathleen Calabrese, Ph.D., is a psychotherapist/hypnotherapist with a private practice in New York City. She conducts creativity and spiritual development workshops and, most recently, has joined the corporate consulting world where she launched a mentoring project for Morgan Stanley IT and served as an executive coach. She can be contacted at kcalabrese@rcn.com.

Empowerment and Self-managing Teams

Connie Wolf

Having followed a typical path to learning management skills, I spent my early career in the traditional hierarchical approach in the work environment. I followed a business administration curriculum in school, took company classes when offered, read books on management and progressed up the corporate ladder absorbing what I could from my managers and from personal experience.

During the late 1980s and early 1990s, however, the world of work began to change dramatically, as computer e-mails within the global company greatly enhanced communication, and information became much more accessible to all employees. Quality improvement processes had led to process improvement and, later, integrated work processes. With so much information available and restructuring becoming a common occurrence, managers were getting overloaded and overstressed. It became apparent that they needed to look at their management style in a whole new way. The culture shift to EMPOWERMENT was born. Managers could no longer handle the span of control, the abundance of information coming their way, and the desire of younger managers to have more responsibility.

At that time, I was in Europe as vice president of human resources and communications for a large company. In addition to leading two separate departments, I was a key resource on the task forces for our internal change efforts and the coordination of the company's Chapter 11 efforts in Europe. My belief always was that good people rise to the level to which they are challenged. I found this to be the time to try out a new approach to handling my responsibilities. I was fortunate to have been able to build my departments with highly talented people. Now was the time to let them perform and grow.

I initiated a process to turn my departments into self-managing teams and empowered the managers in each department to begin a process of shared team development. As we had decided, the managers met regularly, usually without me, to run the operations of their respective departments. Beginning with team development meetings, they determined how they would work and communicate together. They quickly developed their annual plans, which were aligned to department and organizational goals, and met with me for final input and approval. Thereafter, they made decisions, resolved issues among themselves, and invited me to their meetings only as needed. I met with the leaders regularly for updates and made myself available if department members desired to see me.

The lesson I learned through this approach was that people can rise to expectations set for them. The managers who reported to me were experienced professionals who were never given a chance to live up to their potential. They enjoyed the challenge, took greater pride in their work, became high-performing teams, and produced more with greater creativity. I also was able to devote more time to the key strategic issues facing the company at the time. While succeeding in decreasing my daily e-mails and meetings, utilizing self-managing teams also proved to be an excellent development opportunity for my staff. Morale was at an all-time high, despite the fact that we were in Chapter 11.

There are now many books supporting empowerment and participation. Still, many companies are reluctant to give it a try. Women in business need to take risks to find their own style of leadership. By trusting my people, keeping an open communication path, and letting them rise to the challenge, I built two exceptional teams that became the envy of the whole corporation. I challenge all leaders to find ways to let go of the antiquated models of management and to empower future leaders.

# # #

Connie Wolf, MSOD, PCC, is president of Sounding Board®, a service of CBW, Inc. A professional certified coach and consultant, Connie uses her thirty years of corporate experience to assist leaders and individuals in enhancing their effectiveness in business and in life. She can be reached at consultcbw@aol.com or at her Web site: www.SoundingBoardcbw.com.

Section V

Communicate Effectively!

Communicate Effectively!

Joan Eleanor Gustafson

Several years ago, I accepted an exciting, newly created leadership position focused on the development and implementation of new communications technologies to be used within a large global company. I felt fortunate that I would be able to hire forty-nine people to carry out the vision; however, one of the first responsibilities in this position was to outsource the duties of 152 people, who were in communications related roles. Many of the current employees had worked for the company for more than twenty years and had never even considered the possibility of working for another company. My heart went out to them when, upon hearing the news, they went through every emotion possible.

As with all leadership situations, communication was of utmost importance during this critical time. Although many employees did not contact me at first, I knew they had countless questions on their minds. Will I be able to get a job in the new organization? What will happen to me if I don't? Will I be able to find another job in this company? If I don't, what will happen to my pension? Who is Joan Gustafson? Why is she here? Can I trust her? Who made this decision, and why? How do I go about writing a resume? How do I find people who will interview me? Are my skills transferable to another type of job? If I don't find a job in the company, will I get some severance pay? Who will help me? The list went on and on.

I started by making a list of their potential questions and then met first with groups of supervisors and with groups of employees. At first, I opened the jobs in the new department only to these people, and asked them to apply for any they thought might be a fit for them. I also met individually with anyone who requested a meeting with me and, when not in meetings, left my door open for anyone who might want to stop by. I brought in specialists in different functions to answer questions that I was not able to answer. I also sent out daily and weekly updates through e-mail. Although this was not enough to calm their fears, most of the employees gradually began to realize that I cared enough about them to listen and to give them answers. Also, we were able to place most of the employees either in the new department, in another department in the company, or with the vendors to whom we outsourced the work.

Effective communication helps build trust. To be successful, leaders need to make communication a priority and to create a receptive environment. It is important that leaders communicate often, using several media. The fact that a memo or an e-mail message has been sent doesn't mean that the leader has communicated. For communication to take place, there needs to be a mutual understanding.

It is necessary to also be consistent in communicating. After the Dayton's department store chain, headquartered in Minneapolis, Minnesota, merged with the Marshall Field's chain, company management decided to change the name of the Dayton's stores to Marshall Field's. When Linda Ahlers, president of Marshall Field's, was asked by a reporter for *Twin Cities Business Monthly* magazine how the company reassured their customers during this major change, Linda replied that communication was key. She said, "We continued to deliver a single core message: Everything you loved about Dayton's, you're going to love about Marshall Field's. We were known for community giving, for having fashion leadership, for having service that is a cut above other department stores—this wasn't going to change. What was going to change was that we were going to take our company and strategy to the next level."

Listening is the most important communication skill. Listening is an active sport, which requires concentration, asking questions, and giving thoughtful responses. Listen not only to what is said but also to what is meant. People will often have difficulty in finding the right words to express their thoughts. Not only do effective leaders clearly articulate their thoughts, ideas and vision, but also they understand, appreciate, and translate the inarticulate ideas of others. They "listen" to facial expressions, gestures, posture, and other cues that can relay a message. In this section, Patti Cain-Stanley ("Leadership . . . It's All about the Receiver") tells how her career skyrocketed after she learned the art of listening, and Dr. Jeanne Notto Elnadry ("A Physician's Thoughts on Leadership") discusses her lessons in listening while serving as a physician in a tiny hospital in Arizona.

In my experience, over-communication does not exist, and I encourage you to communicate, and then to communicate and to communicate some more.

This section of the book contains some excellent recommendations on communication from five female leaders. Having a sense of humor is essential to leadership, according to Debra Benton in "Women Who Lead with Levity." In "Different Rules," Jean Hollands encourages women to use a softer inter-relational touch in business. Linda Herold ("Accidental Leadership") then takes communication to another level by communicating to others through her actions.

The recommendations from the leaders featured in this section will help you to become an even better leader than you are now. As Charles Darwin said, "In the long history of humankind (and animalkind, too), those who learned to collaborate . . . most effectively have prevailed."

Leadership . . . It's All about the Receiver

Patti Cain-Stanley

All my life, I've been leading people, either formally or informally. Frankly, I think this is because I am bossy and can out-talk (or wear-out) most people. Good or bad, this "talent" has put me at the forefront of most activities in which I am involved. However, just because one has the mantle, this does not assure effectiveness. Although there are many components to strong leadership, one has stood out among the rest for me. It is an orientation and a way of communicating that leads people to follow, and to follow strongly. Simply, it is a focus on the receiver.

My motley leadership story began when I was twenty-one, recently out of college, and fresh out of a nine-month management-training program. I was given my first leadership assignment . . . to manage a $2.1 million catalog department with twenty-one employees, a call center, and a retail storefront. Trainees were never given a first assignment of this size, but circumstances and strong test scores paved the way. I stayed in the back room all day analyzing reports to find ways to improve profits. I thought that locked somewhere in that data would be the key; eventually I would find it.

My only connection with my team was when I was called to the front to handle a customer issue. I continued this pattern of behavior for a year. I was terrible!

Mercifully for everyone, I transitioned out of leading people when I moved away and took a job in marketing with AT&T. Marketing was really a euphemism for sales, but I didn't know that when I took the job. Never had I dreamed of a sales job . . . too negative a connotation! Besides, I didn't kill myself in school to hawk some merchandise to unsuspecting dupes. However, despite my initial reservations, I liked the company, the people were nice, and I was learning something new. So, for three years, I worked at convincing business people, who were fifteen- to forty-years older than me, to purchase communications systems that were priced between $100,000 and $500,000. Again, I was not initially very good, but I got better—a lot better.

I was young and the sole provider for my family while my husband pursued his education. I couldn't imagine failing so soon in my career and was determined to figure out the sales game. Luckily, there were some seasoned sales professionals who were kind enough to let me tag along while they worked their communications magic. Despite trip after trip, nothing I saw looked particularly earth shattering or inherently different from my approach. Yet, I continued to toil away at only 33 percent of my sales goal while they were at 200 percent. Clearly, I was not able to glean the important elements through observation. Like Dorothy in *The Wizard of Oz*, I had to learn it on my own.

Sometime during my second year, I began understanding the key that would propel me forward throughout my career as a salesperson, as a leader of organizations, and as an executive coach. As with most insights, it would turn out to be staggering in its simplicity. Thousands of books have been written on the topic of leadership, and I've read a nice subset of these; however, I was apparently too caught up in me to allow this truth to resonate.

What truth is that? Whether selling a product, service, idea or concept, effective communication is about the *receiver.* Again, on the surface, this is nothing earth shattering; however, when truly applied, its power is limitless. Once my "aha" was fully evolved, I stopped trying to sell or convince people, but began to communicate, starting from their vantage point. My new approach included lots of questions, lots of generous listening, and lots of creating space for my customers to express their needs, wishes, and desires. Within six months of this realization, my sales improved 220 percent. I had saved my job and adopted a way of being which became the platform for even greater performance and the insight for how to effectively lead.

A year later, at age twenty-five, I was chosen from among thirty peers to be the first of our start-up group to move into a sales manager position. For some reason, I saw this position as fundamentally different from my sales position. It's easy for us to compartmentalize and not see the applicability of past skill sets. For me, sales leadership was something totally divergent from direct sales. Certainly, I was going to be leading people who sold, but I didn't see that I had brought with me an essential skill for leadership. Fortunately for me, I had a mentor who helped me connect the dots.

Having a mentor was not a planned move. I had fallen into it, but it would prove to be pivotal. For two days prior to taking on my new role, my mentor gave me all he could on sales management, but, even more important, on leadership. If I were to be the most effective sales manager there was, what would I look like? He had me answer that question from the sales person's point of view. If my new team were to have a choice of any sales manager living, would they choose me? Would my new boss choose me? How would I make sure that my clients (team, boss, peers, etc.) were satisfied? Who would I need to be? How would I need to communicate? I would need to be able to always keep those questions in the front of my mind, guiding my actions, if I were to be the best I could be for the people I supported and served.

This was pretty heady stuff for someone my age, but the wisdom of it was unmistakable. You need to always act as if you are a business of one and to always act as though people have an option to work with you or not. Remember, literally or figuratively, they do have that option and they will eventually exercise it, whether directly or indirectly, by tuning you out, working around you, subverting your work, etc. We need to attract people to our work and our message. Certainly we need competency in what we do, but how we do it, the process of support and communication, is up to us. How often do we try to move our position forward without regard to whether it serves the other person? How much easier would it be to make things happen if we looked for a way for the receiver of the message or service to feel supremely important, cared for, listened to, recognized, and valued?

Still, this doesn't sound like a silver bullet . . . too simple, too dull. However, if I had not gotten in front of that sales team and spent two hours telling them how I'd support them instead of what they were going to do for me, I know I wouldn't have been the AT&T #2 SMB sales manager in the nation my first year, at age twenty-five, in Manhattan, with a team of five kids who had never sold and one seasoned player. I succeeded in this because I inspired, supported, teamed, worked, developed and set high standards for us all to live up to. Every week I gave them something new. I looked to develop them, and, in turn, I was constantly developing myself. I received a "Best Boss" nomination from my team and went to the Millionaire's Club. I did the same the following year and the next, and then moved up the corporate ladder to vice president at age thirty-seven.

Whether selling an idea as a leader of a business or being a one-person shop selling yourself, it is all about the receiver and what they want. The key is finding a way to create an environment for everyone to win on some level. Later, before I got in front of my team or organization to deliver any message, I stood where they would be and looked through their eyes at who I was being (how I came off) and my message. If it didn't resonate, I threw it out. Often I would design a message that communicated what I needed to communicate, but not in a manner that the receiver might be able to hear it. If it was not going to be effective, I did not hesitate to dispose of it. They were buying my service, and I was there to support them. Who did I need to be? It's funny how the upside down pyramid (flipping the notion of hierarchies) really does create a paradigm shift. It opens people up to being the best they can be and to bring that out in others.

Seventeen years later, that principle has served me more than any other. Certainly you need a fair amount of skill, training, experience, etc., but the notion that my team (insert whomever I support) could fire me at anytime, overtly or otherwise, moved me to stay in a continuous learning mode with a customer focus. My communication supported that orientation—focus on the receiver. Today, as an executive coach, I utilize these lessons that helped forge my success, to listen to and support people in the manner they seek and very much deserve. Most of the time, as a one-woman band, I'm back to those initial days as a salesperson. It's even harder now, because the product I sell is myself. I need to be able to concentrate on the individual, the receiver, and what this individual needs. The rest will follow. And it has.

# # #

Patti Cain-Stanley is an executive coach and business leadership consultant to corporate leaders and their teams. As a former executive with a technology start-up and a major communications firm, Patti was drawn to the coaching profession when she herself achieved breakthrough performance through the support of a coach. Today, Patti coaches on myriad topics, but invariably finds ineffective communication to be a central challenge to managerial and executive effectiveness.

A Physician's Thoughts on Leadership

Jeanne Notto Elnadry, M.D.

Since I was twelve years old, I have understood that if I am not happy about something, I am responsible to change myself or my situation to make it better. I don't need to wait until someone does it for me. This realization, which came to me suddenly one day when I was walking down the hall between classes at my junior high school, has defined much of my life.

A "born leader" I am not. I am a quiet, private person, always a little uncomfortable being in the spotlight. I often tell my patients not to put me on too high a pedestal in their minds—if I fall, it's a long way down to the bottom.

Becoming a leader has been an evolutionary process for me. Often, chance has had as much influence as planning and design. My first career in nursing did not give me the degree of control I hoped to attain, but, nevertheless, it gave me an excellent foundation in interpersonal skills. I later chose to study medicine, so I could give the orders and influence decisions, rather than being required to only follow orders. (Nursing has evolved greatly since I left the profession, and now nurses have much greater influence in the care of their patients.) After finishing medical school, with all the careful planning for a new career with a combined internal medicine and pediatric specialty, chance intervened again when I suddenly found myself a young widow halfway through an internal medicine residency. Instead of remaining on the East Coast as I had planned, I was drawn to Arizona. (I believe this was directly related to reading *Arizona Highways*, a magazine to which my father had subscribed during the years I was growing up). After carefully negotiating a contract with a large HMO in Baltimore, which included tuition paid for two years for a master of public health degree at Johns Hopkins University, I canceled everything and left for Arizona to work in a tiny hospital on an Indian reservation in the southwestern corner of the state.

In this little hospital with its busy clinic, I spent four years refining my skills while taking care of very complex medical patients. Indeed, I believe one very important aspect of leadership is to have a high level of skill in one's chosen area. However, the most important lesson I learned at Fort Yuma Indian Hospital is the importance of hearing all sides when there is a concern or dispute and, likewise, the necessity to have a method of independently verifying the truth or completeness of the information given. I found myself in trouble many times for believing one person, taking action based on that information, and later learning that I had been told only part of the story. These experiences helped me to learn the value of following principles, such as fairness and justice.

It has taken many years for me to find my niche in the professional world. My work now as a specialist in hospice and palliative medicine is very satisfying. Since there are fewer than 800 physicians certified in hospice and palliative medicine in this country, the opportunities for service are enormous. I am now developing a palliative medicine consultation service at our only hospital in Yuma, Arizona, to serve the needs of people who are dying and to reduce the suffering of patients and their families at the end of life. I have a busy private practice with a diverse patient population.

Along the way, I have learned a number of principles that I believe are important to becoming an effective leader. Having a charismatic personality is not one of them! Of course, all of us know a few charismatic personalities who are inspiring and are admired by many. However, most of us are fairly ordinary people, and yet we can be effective leaders too.

1. Provide the very best service possible. Focus on service first, and money second. I attribute this principle to observing my dad's lifelong contributions to the development of electronic commerce, from the earliest stage of envisioning the possibilities to the current stage of electronic commerce across many industries.

2. Always do your best.

3. Envision your goal. Have clear goals in mind, but, at the same time, be flexible enough to adapt to changing circumstances.

4. Be consistent.

5. Have high standards, and be the first to uphold them.

6. Help others along the way to become empowered themselves.

7. Don't burn any bridges. Always build bridges, and try to bring together people from different areas. Having people who can look at a problem from many different perspectives enhances creativity.

8. Stay away from political squabbling within your organization; maintain harmonious, or at least civil, relationships with everyone.

9. Seek to resolve conflict creatively in a way that everyone benefits. Allow others to "save face." No one appreciates being humiliated. "People will forget what you did; people will forget what you said; but people will never forget how you made them feel." (I don't know the author of this statement, but I believe it.)

10. When you are right, refrain from saying, "I told you so."

11. Recognize that change takes time. Have patience as people go through the process of recognizing a need, learning what they can do, and eventually making changes in behavior.

12. Patiently educate. Help the "learner" to feel good about her-self/himself by noting what she/he is doing well, and build on that.

13. Know yourself, your strengths and your shortcomings. Work in an environment that enhances your strengths. For example, I know I am more effective as a leader in a small- to medium-sized organization, where I know most of the people, and I can "put my arms around" the system. It is small enough that I can understand it and work with it.

14. Develop a balance between personal and professional life, and between the spiritual and intellectual life. Allow time for reflection. This nurtures the soul and stimulates creativity.

No matter where we wish to exercise our leadership skills, we should understand what is important and what is most important. I believe that our families are most important, and often sacrifices are needed to keep families intact and functioning well as nurturing units. When we leave this earth, we do not take our titles or programs or budgets with us. What we leave behind are the relationships we have with those we care about, the memories of how we treated people along the way, and the caring we have brought to our work and play every day.

# # #

Dr. Jeanne Notto Elnadry is a physician, specializing in hospice and palliative medicine. She is currently developing a palliative medicine consultation service at the hospital in Yuma, Arizona, to serve the needs of people who are dying and to reduce the suffering of patients and their families at the end of life.

Women Who Lead with Levity

Debra Benton

Women who lead with levity, lead well and lead long. Women who attempt to lead without levity eventually fail measurably . . . and miserably.

I have worked with many powerful women. To put it simply: I've enjoyed, valued, and respected the ones who have an attitude of good cheer about themselves and about life. I have *not* enjoyed, valued, or liked the ones without this attitude. (By the way, I feel the same way about men.) Often I respect their competence, but that is not enough to succeed in a competitive work environment where you (and I) could be replaced tomorrow.

I have worked with many powerful men, too. To put it simply: they enjoy, value, and respect a woman who is good at her work *but* also displays an attitude of good cheer about herself and life. They do not enjoy, value, or like a woman who carries some form of "chip on her shoulder." (If you happen to be very attractive they might give you a "grace period" in working with them just so they can look, and sometimes just leer at you longer, but they will not consider you a serious player, much less a leader.)

To lead, you must have and display a sense of humor. Let me correct myself: at least you have to *display* it. I don't care if you really have it. Although it's pretty tough to fake, I've known both women and men who have succeeded in doing it. (It's not too dissimilar from faking self-confidence or competence—something we all have done at one time or another in our life.) What's important for our discussion right now is that you grasp the incredible significance of displaying fun in your serious work.

When Pepsi-Cola executives are gathered in a boardroom strategizing an inroad into the multi-billion-dollar China market to counteract the Coca-Cola invasion, eventually one person will ease the tension in the room by joking, "Let's not go overboard here, we're just talking about bottled sugar water." Although not necessarily a line Jay Leno would use, that one line in this situation is enough levity to reduce the stress, put things in perspective, and cause clearer thinking.

Mindy Credi, a people development expert, says, "Growing up around my grandmother and mother, I learned to use humor in dealing with family issues. I remember one of my Italian grandmother's favorite sayings, 'Melinda, don't-ah spit-ah into the wind-ah.' But I never thought women could use humor in business. It wasn't until many years into my career when I worked with the first female president of Pepsi-Cola and I saw her: a company president, a leader, a woman who had accomplished a lot, and she had a great sense of humor. She was always kidding people about things, even with her boss, in important meetings."

To display humor:

- Have an attitude of good cheer and keep it despite what happens.
- Be around good-natured people who are also productive and hard working (you know, like yourself).
- Don't engage in the negative involving people or situations.
- Look like a winner in your comportment/posture, i.e., like you have the "world by the tail" rather than "the weight of the world on your shoulders."
- Be consistent in using humor with everyone you meet.
- Don't fret if you don't get roars of laughter. (They are probably holding it inside.)

- When you laugh, always laugh, don't giggle. Girls giggle. Female leaders laugh.

If you are a woman who injects appropriate humor into important business situations, you will be praised, honored, respected, and hoisted onto pedestals. Well, okay, maybe I went a little overboard on the last one, but at the very least you will be allowed to stay and play in the game. And if you want to lead, you have to be in the game. As you will learn, people will allow you to lead them only if you make it enjoyable for them to follow.

#

Debra Benton, president of Benton Management Resources, Inc., Fort Collins, Colorado, is an international speaker, executive coach, and award-winning author of several best-selling books that include *How to Think Like a CEO* (Warner Books), *How to Act Like a CEO* (McGraw-Hill), *Secrets of a CEO Coach* (McGraw-Hill), and *Lions Don't Need to Roar* (Warner Books). Debra can be contacted at Debra@TopSpeaker.com.

Different Rules

Jean Hollands

Women were born with the eagerness to attach and to make others comfortable. In order to do that, we learned fabulous multi-tasking skills. We can entertain the foreign sales representatives while comforting the secretary on the way out the door. We can remember to send roses for husband to his mother, to copy the soccer schedule, and to pick up the juice bars for the T-ball game.

Men, of course, as children seem more uni-focused on getting something rolling—a ball, a teddy bear, the mallet from the Tinker Toy set. Just get them something to roll! I watched the difference between two granddaughters as they began to crawl and move about. My three grandsons would begin to pound something the moment they could grab, and they would push anything at all. The girls tended to want to relate—to move toward another baby or soft cuddly toy. Of course, there are exceptions.

The difference between men and women in conflict is quite interesting. Men still seem to do the "flight or fight" response. Women do the "tend or befriend" response. They want to fix something or someone, or they want to repair or "make nice" with their adversary.

This "tend or befriend" response was recently determined in a UCLA research study about patterns between men and women. In my experience, neither gender likes disagreements, but women seem to take them more personally and can, in fact, become more deeply wounded and suffer longer.

Even if we are not born with the softer inter-relational touch, we are inculcated with a 500-year culture wherein men did the hunting while women did the gathering and camp tending. Now that women are in the business world, having to get our own buffalo, we are learning that we actually have to sharpen our tools. Sometimes we are pretty clumsy at it; thus, my book, *Same Game, Different Rules*.

There are twenty-five rules in all, including:

- Create allies (lots of them).
- Don't burn bridges—ever.
- Wait for apologies, but don't wait to make some.
- You can't control everything.
- Soft sell is the best sell.
- Don't judge—enjoy.
- Success starts inside.

For women in business, it is necessary to equip themselves with the soft touch, even in hard times. Do this, and you'll be on the road to more success as a leader.

# # #

Jean A. Hollands is founder and CEO of Growth and Leadership Center (GLC), which serves many Fortune 100 companies as well as smaller start-ups. With executive coaching as its mainstream product, GLC is an innovator in the field of executive and leadership development.

Jean is a sought-after keynote speaker and is frequently featured on television and radio and in the print media. She is the author of four books and numerous articles. She is the recipient of the 1996 Athena Award, three Business Woman of the Year awards, the Blue Chip Entrepreneurial Award, and several others. For more information, visit Jean's Web site at www.glcweb.com.

Accidental Leadership

Linda M. Herold

Leadership has been both a puzzle and a privilege for me. The puzzle, quite simply, is "why me?" Every day, I encounter gifted, talented, successful women from all walks of life, who are leaders in their own right. Yet they seek direction and leadership from me in developing a fuller, more engaged and enjoyable way of living. What happened is that on the way to creating a new women's networking community, I discovered that my messages of beauty, kindness, and high personal standards resonated with others in a special way. In order to solve the puzzle of how that happened, I had to take a long look back at myself.

My own lack of nurturing early in life created a need in me to care for and about others. Helping others and giving back to the community are simply part of my operating principals. I could not have reached my goals without them. However, what I give back that others seem to appreciate most is a sense of identity. A clear understanding, a knowing of the elements of my own identity, is what I believe has attracted others to my leadership style. My identity is the example. Helping others create an identity is the goal. Let me explain.

Identity is the message we send, and it must serve our goals and ambitions. Who am I? To a large extent, it's a choice to be made, not just a given to be accepted and dealt with. Is this the life I really want, or do I desire to invent the future? My message is that life isn't about finding yourself; life is about creating yourself.

Heredity is a given, of course, but the visual, vocal, and verbal arts which define us can be acquired. After all, education, social graces, culture, and style are all part of self-development. Choices are many. We evaluate opportunities and implement those choices. To promote our identity, we entertain ideas, explore information, seek resources, and evaluate concepts, each in our own unique way. Each player in the game of life can perform well or poorly. My leadership role is to be the coach and cheering section rolled into one.

While I am humbled by the mantle of leadership that others have chosen to bestow on me, I am also thrilled by it. It is a privilege and a pleasure to serve my community. The sense of possibility I seem to awaken in others reflects back on me. It encourages me to work even harder to bring people together in harmonious and mutually beneficial ways.

There is a flow to the leadership experience. It is not a chore, nor a duty. Leadership is its own reward.

# # #

Linda M. Herold is president of Herold Enterprises, which consists of three components that work together harmoniously. *The Herold Report*, a quarterly journal, provides a forum for promoting women in the metro Phoenix area. Women of Scottsdale sponsors well-attended monthly luncheons with a social as well as a business agenda. Identity Arts assists individuals in the art of creating and managing their images and reputations in the business community. Linda is dedicated to helping others and has received numerous awards, including "The Spirit of Women" award and "Small Business Journalist of the Year."

Section VI

Set High Standards, and Live Accordingly!

Set High Standards, and Live Accordingly!

Joan Eleanor Gustafson

In my research on success and leadership, I asked effective female leaders to rate each of several leadership characteristics and qualities on a scale of one to five, with "five" meaning that the characteristic or quality was extremely important. One hundred percent of the women rated integrity as a "five."

Integrity is more than just honesty. Each leader defines integrity in a slightly different way. For me, it includes a strong degree of commitment. If I say I am going to do something, I do it. I don't say I am going to do something because I have "good intentions" of doing it or because I think it is what the listener wants to hear. If I say it, I do it. For example, if I say to someone, "Let's get together for lunch," I look at my calendar and schedule the lunch. One of my personal standards is that my word is my bond. Integrity and commitment go hand in hand.

When I interviewed Jill Lublin, international speaker and author of *Guerrilla Publicity*, she commented on the importance of keeping commitments. She said that an important component of effective leadership is getting out of bed on days that you don't feel like it. An entrepreneur throughout most of her career, she knows that staying on schedule is important. "You have to be disciplined in your schedule. As an entrepreneur, it's very easy to get sidetracked or pulled away to handle the most important crisis of the minute," she said. If Jill makes an appointment to meet with someone, either in person or on the phone, she keeps that commitment and is there exactly when she said she would be there. This is part of her integrity—a standard that she lives each day.

In *Principle-Centered Leadership*, Stephen Covey says that integrity is "honestly matching words and feelings with thoughts and actions." This, again, has to do with keeping commitments.

Linda Chandler is a dynamic inspirational speaker, who speaks often of the importance of "P-I-G," an acronym she pegged for persistence, integrity, and guts. These three qualities have contributed significantly to her success as a leader and to the success of those she has mentored. The word "commitment" is very high in her vocabulary list. She told me that when she was leading a new project for people of another culture who had some biases against her at first, she let them know that she was making promises to them that she would keep. "I kept those promises, from the little ones to the big ones, step-by-step," she said. "I learned to build trust very quickly, and this opened the lines of communication. I honored these people and respected what they told me." While doing this, she built leaders in that community, and these leaders now honor her for her high standards and integrity in living these standards.

The leaders in this section give their insights and examples related to values, character, and integrity. Julie Davis ("Tools for Successful Leadership") discusses the values she learned growing up on a farm and the importance of these values in the business world. Beth mAcdonald ("To Thine Own Self Be True") speaks of the importance of knowing oneself and the spiritual dimension of leadership. Then Dr. Audri Lanford ("Eight Principles for True Leadership") shares her values, which have helped her to become a successful leader.

As is evidenced by these writings, part of personal integrity is to know oneself and to be oneself. True leaders know themselves, both their strengths and their weaknesses, and they don't lie to themselves. They are dedicated to honest thoughts and actions.

Stephen Covey says, "When we are true to the light we have been given, when we keep our word consistently, when we are striving continually to harmonize our habit system with our value system, then our honor system becomes greater than our moods, and we can have confidence in ourselves because we know ourselves."

Through living their standards, leaders inspire trust. Knowing that "talking the talk" is not enough, they are role models for others by "walking the talk." They set an example and model behavior in a positive and professional manner.

Personal integrity is a personal choice. As a woman increases her level of integrity, she begins to become aware of the following in her life:

- She has more energy.
- She feels effortless about achieving her desired results.
- She feels much less stress in her life.
- She attracts into her life more fulfilling people who are consistently reliable, empowering, loving, and inspiring.
- She enjoys a richer and more successful life.
- As a leader, she becomes more effective.

In *Golden Nuggets*, Sir John Templeton says, "Probably the greatest secret to peace of mind is living the life of personal integrity—not what people think of you, but what you know of yourself. If you remain true to your ethical principles, your personal integrity can become an attractive beacon for success on every level."

May your integrity be an attractive beacon for your own success as a leader!

Tools for Successful Leadership

Julie Davis

When asked recently to give the commencement address at Kansas State University where I had graduated years ago, I was greatly flattered. It was a sense of déjà vu. Twenty-three years earlier, as the senior class president, I had addressed my own graduating class at the KSU commencement exercises. My thoughts immediately went back to my message at that time, which had focused on what my classmates and I had learned during the first twenty-two or twenty-three years of our lives. It seemed only fitting that I would focus my remarks this year on what I had learned in the twenty-three years since then.

Once I got past the initial flattery of being asked, I set about the much more difficult task of deciding what I might say that would be—according to the dean's charge—profound, likely to shape lives, and completed within fifteen minutes! No small job! In fact, as often as I make speeches as part of my professional responsibilities, this particular one seemed far more challenging—and important.

I soon realized that there was nothing I could say to these graduating seniors that would be as profound, or as life-changing, as the experiences they'd already had, both at K-State and in their years growing up. Indeed, despite all the miles I had traveled, both literally and figuratively, since my own graduation, there was nothing that I had learned that was more important to me or my future success than what I already knew at the time I graduated. Like those graduating seniors, I already had all the tools for success at the time I walked off campus. Those tools have since formed a foundation and served as a touchstone throughout my entire career. Those tools—then and now—consisted of an understanding that values matter, character counts, and success is not forever.

Values matter

No matter where I've lived or how far I've traveled, I've never strayed far from the Midwestern values that I hold dear. For me, those values were shaped by growing up within a Kansas farm family. Regardless of background, though, I see those same values among my successful business colleagues. The three values that have become the most important to me in the business world are stewardship, perseverance, and self-sufficiency.

Stewardship

Growing up on a farm, I learned that stewardship meant taking care of the land and the equipment so that it could be passed down from one generation to the next—over and over again. The same thing should be true in the business world. Regardless of what our job descriptions may read, we are all stewards. The most successful corporate leaders in America today are those who have been mindful of their responsibilities of stewardship. They look beyond quarterly earnings. They—and we—have learned that it is not enough to merely preserve and protect those assets entrusted to our care. We must nurture them and enhance their value before passing them on at the expiration of our trusteeship.

Perseverance

On the farm, perseverance meant getting up every morning, through rain or shine, and doing the job. Farming meant planting a crop every fall, even when the year before had been hailed out. We've all learned that there are hailstorms in the business world, too. Things don't go according to plan. There will be setbacks. We must learn to persevere and lead, even in those times of adversity.

Self-sufficiency

On the farm, self-sufficiency meant taking responsibility for getting your job done—whatever that job was. In business, it takes on a little different meaning—especially in this age of free agency. The days of the company man/woman are gone. No one starting a career today expects to retire with a gold watch after thirty years of service with the same company. Acting as a free agent, we must each accept responsibility for looking after our own career. If we don't, who will?

Character counts

There is currently a popular book entitled *Character is Destiny*, and it's required reading in some organizations. To understand its message, though, one needs to know what character is. Character is the kind of person you are inside; your personal code of ethics; the sum total of your habits, values, virtues, and vices. Character is important because one's long-term success will not ride on what he or she knows, but on the strength of his/her character. It is the differentiator between those leaders who will succeed long-term and those who won't. In large part, it determines the shape, quality, and direction of one's life.

How does one measure character? It can be said that character is *what do we do when we know no one else will know what we do*. Character is what we do when no one else is looking. So the hard part is not in *knowing* what is right but in *doing* what is right. It is not enough to just say no to what is wrong. Our goal must be to say yes to what is right. I learned from my farming background that pulling weeds does not by itself make for a beautiful garden or a healthy crop. One must do the things that are *right*, as well—planting, watering, and fertilizing.

Success is not forever

As leaders, each of us has grown accustomed to success. We live in a society that celebrates success. No one ever talks about failure. However, *staying* successful is far more challenging than *being* successful. We read it in our own company prospectus, which says, "Past performance is no guarantee of future results." This is as true for people as it is for corporations.

When will we learn that no one expects us to finish first every time? When will we learn that failure is important, too? Well-known business author, Tom Peters, says corporations should actually reward people for failure, because failure means risk; and without risk there can be no success.

What will be important to us as leaders is what we do when we experience failure. After all, sooner or later, every leader will fail at something. For some, that will be a big, ugly, public and humiliating experience.

Failure affects people differently. For some, it is tempting to dive under the desk, to quit, or to hide. Others, including the successful leaders among us, use failure to motivate themselves to overcome the disappointment and the discouragement and move on. Those leaders understand that most failures are only temporary defeats that can be converted into priceless assets.

For the sake of our younger colleagues, we can hope that they experience failure early in their development as leaders. I was thirty-nine years old before I experienced my first really big, ugly, public and humiliating failure. I wish now it had happened earlier. I would then have had the benefit of what I learned from that experience much sooner in my career.

Closing thoughts on leadership

We see the world not as it is, but as we are. As leaders, it is important to understand that our perspectives are shaped by our values and our character. It is important to understand that we'll not win every race. We must lead by example. We must set high standards and live accordingly. The world around us is watching.

# # #

Julie L. Davis is the managing partner of Andersen's worldwide Intellectual Asset Consulting practice. Over the last ten years she has been asked to testify in several of the largest infringement law-suits in America. Julie speaks frequently on the topic of intellectual property and has co-authored a widely praised book titled *Edison in the Boardroom: How Leading Companies Realize Value from their Intellectual Assets.*

To Thine Own Self Be True

Beth mAcdonald

Knowing who you are, and realizing that knowing who you are is a never-ending process, are the two most important discoveries of my thirty years of leadership experience.

As an enthusiastic young scientist at Johnson & Johnson, I found myself surrounded by men. I like men, so that was a good thing. In subtle ways, however, I received the message that men are the leaders, and so I began, unknowingly, to modify my own behavior to become more leader-like, more manlike. Of course, there's no mistaking me for a man, so the result was androgyny, and the energy I projected was confused. Over time, I have been learning to reclaim the power of my feminine energy. The trick is figuring out how to hang onto all that useful male perspective at the same time!

Today, with the emphasis on emotional intelligence and the desire to transcend intellect to tap intuition, the "feminine skills" have greater corporate value. Decades of diversity training and tomes full of equal opportunity laws have had an impact, at least in the U.S. and European environments, so the issue of maintaining your feminine identity in the workplace is not as great. The focus shifts to a more universally human discovery of self.

What does knowing yourself have to do with your ability to lead? Well, whom do you want to follow? Most of us want to follow someone who:

- knows where she's going.
- tells the truth.
- knows her own limits and capabilities.
- has a clear sense of morality and ethics.
- has compassion and a spiritual dimension.

In other words, most of us want to follow someone who knows who she is. There is no one more powerful than a person who acts from conviction, with passion and self-knowledge. This is the person who becomes larger than life in our worlds. These are the people who become our leaders and our heroines.

For many of us women, knowing where we are going is intuitive and undeclared. I am learning that leadership requires me to describe my destination clearly. In addition, I am discovering that I am most compelling when I describe that destination in many ways: visually, rationally, emotionally, on paper, orally and even, if I can, kinesthetically. It is almost as though I am building a mental reality. The more complete I can make that mental reality, the more compelling it is to other people.

When someone tells the truth, a deep meaningful truth, I feel it. Sometimes the hair on my arms stands up. Sometimes it is a feeling like an electric current passing through my body. Sometimes it is simply a sense of surety, a feeling of comfort. I am learning that when I can find those deep and meaningful truths and have the courage to express them, I can connect to other people; I inspire other people; and people listen to what I am saying. Sometimes, they follow me.

One of my most deeply held beliefs is that we all have amazing, untapped reservoirs of talent and knowledge. The evidence of these reservoirs has come from many places. Neuroscientists explain how little of our brains we actually use. Physicians describe remarkable recoveries from brain injuries that should have left patients mentally crippled; instead, they simply shifted to another part of their brain. Practitioners of ancient arts like qi gong, yoga, or the martial arts perform remarkable mental and physical feats. I am convinced that we can tap into some mysterious reservoir of capability and do remarkable things.

I am finding that one of the most important roles of a leader is to plug into that reservoir, not only in order to access its power, but also to provide an example that will allow other people to discover their own potential.

For me, "limits" is an uncomfortable word. I prefer to re-conceptualize it in another way. I like to imagine that I am connected to everything, to everyone. I like to imagine that I am a very special being with particular talents. I am most powerful *and* the system is most powerful, when I capitalize on those unique talents and draw on the unique talents of other people. Although we are connected, we aren't interchangeable. Each of us has a special role. I need to discover that special role and focus on being the best that I can in that role. Recognizing my own talents, and how they differ from the talents of others, guides my decisions and informs my leadership.

More than a decade of my life has been spent in Asia. This exposure to other cultures has led me to appreciate the distinction between morality and ethics. I believe that moral values are those core human beliefs that transcend culture. On the other hand, ethics are rules of conduct agreed upon by each culture. My friendships and working relationships with people from across Asia, from Europe and South America have led me to conclude that there are core values; there is a universal sense of morality. On the other hand, my American sensibilities have been routinely challenged by the variety of ethical systems I have encountered.

Discovering my own beliefs has been of critical importance, so that I sort out the American biases from the universal values. I feel that this process has strengthened me as a leader. I am sure of my fundamental values, and I try to act from those values. Of course, I often fail, but I try to use my failure to re-examine those values, reaffirm them and renew my commitment. I am acutely aware of how my American upbringing colors my view of the world. I have discovered what I appreciate about my heritage and what I would like to learn and adopt from other cultures. Again, I feel that I am stronger as a leader because I have developed a tolerance of a wide variety of perspectives. I can see a little bit more of the world, and I can understand and connect with other people a little bit better.

Understanding, and connecting with other people, has improved my ability to be compassionate. Compassion is one of the most important leadership qualities in my personal model. The ability to transcend one's self is key to leadership, because, in my model, leadership is not about getting people to do what you personally want, but is about discerning what needs to be done in order to serve those being led.

The spiritual dimension of leadership is the doorway to a very powerful energy. It is the route to that great reservoir of untapped potential. It is the pathway to compassion and to agape, the universal and transcending love that guides leaders to the right path. I believe that there are many ways in which to develop the spiritual dimension. For some people, it is the role of religion. My path includes self-reflection, meditation, and constant exploration of what others are discovering.

I have found that setting aside time for reflection brings me a peace of mind that is critical to me as a leader. Without it, I only manage and direct. Constant growth and renewal are essential to a leader. I truly believe that there are only two options: growth or decay. Leaders must grow, having the courage to face the unknown frontiers of our own psyches. I have accepted that this is a never-ending process; every time I think I know, I discover something I never imagined. I draw energy and excitement from the unending process of self-discovery.

I hope you will, too.

# # #

Trained in textile design and leadership, Beth mAcdonald spent twenty years creating a career in research and development at Johnson & Johnson. She journeyed from a junior scientist position to regional director in a career that focused on the development of the consumer products that millions of people use with trust everyday all around the world. She received numerous awards and acknowledgments for her technical and leadership contributions to industry and for her support of teamwork across cultural and gender barriers.

Beth now lives in the Philippines where she is developing an industrial design business, BraveDesign.net (www.bravedesign.net) and contributing to leadership education through PSI Asia (http://psi-asia.org), a leading source of leadership training in Asia.

Eight Principles for True Leadership

Audri G. Lanford, Ph.D.

I've always been a very independent person—and yes, a leader. My mother loves to tell the story about when I was two-and-a-half years old. She decided to start looking for what was then called a nursery school for me to attend in the future. At the time, I didn't speak any English—my parents were from Germany, as was our nanny, so I spoke only German.

When we visited the first school, I loved it. I told my mother that I wanted to stay. She asked me how I'd get home, and I told her that I'd take the bus with the other children. I sent my mother home—and learned English that day! She was a bit overwhelmed, but decided it was good I was so independent. That hasn't changed over the years. . . .

I'm quite proud of several of my professional accomplishments. The top three include earning a Ph.D. from Stanford University; starting, growing, and selling one of the fastest growing private companies in the United States, an Inc. 500 company, with my husband, Jim; and helping thousands of business people use the Internet profitably—years before that was fashionable.

There are eight principles that I believe are the basis for my success and can help women who wants to develop leadership skills:

1. **Create big dreams.** I love trying to do what others say is impossible. When we started Micro Dynamics, our Inc. 500

189

software company, people thought there was no way a tiny company could compete with $200 million (to many billion dollar) companies—and succeed. Yet, we did. Today, our vision is even bigger. One of our goals is to help a million business owners and professionals become outrageously successful getting more customers and clients. Think big!

2. **Rely on a foundation of honesty and integrity.** I don't just mean not lying, cheating, or stealing. That goes without saying. Instead, I mean making sure that the small decisions—and the ones other people may not even know about—are also based on a foundation of honesty and integrity. It's the small things that make all the difference.

3. **Always provide enormous value.** Our company is dedicated to over-delivering and to exceeding our customers' expectations. I try to focus on making sure that everything we do is rooted in providing our customers with extraordinary value.

4. **Make it fun to do business with you.** I love what we do—and it shows in our corporate culture. We're playful. You can see what I mean on the WZ.com site where we have WZ-ards (pronounced wizards) who share the very best resources about their topic area ("Realm"). Our attorney even wears her WZ-ard hat when she writes our contracts.

5. **Don't worry about the competition.** I never consider the competition—in fact, I don't believe we have any. I like to work with our competitors for the mutual benefit of both companies. For example, when we were co-hosting the Billion Dollar Internet Marketing Summit with Jay Abraham two years ago, I invited our best competitors to speak. It turned out to be the most amazing Internet marketing conference ever. Each of 150 people paid $5,000 to attend, and we sold hundreds of home study programs at $2,000 each. Working with your competitors can be very profitable!

6. **Be a bit outrageous.** You can't do what everyone else is doing—you have to be different—to succeed and be a leader. So, I love to look for ways to be outrageous—especially to market outrageously. I don't mean being a nut. Instead, I'm referring

to doing "out of the box" things that get attention and benefit your customers. You can see an example at www.MoreCustomers.com.

7. **Focus on learning new things.** I've spent a fortune on my education, and I'm not referring to my Ph.D. In fact, when Jim and I moved across the country twenty-two years ago, we blew out three tires on the moving truck because we had so many books! I've literally spent several hundred thousand dollars on books, seminars, audiotape programs, etc. And it is the best investment I've ever made. Why? Because it has helped me earn many, many times that amount for our businesses and myself. Start small—but start.

The keys to making this work for you are to learn from people who are already successful—and to apply what you learn. Always ask yourself, "How can I apply this to *my* business?" And have fun with it. Learning is fun, so enjoy the process.

8. **Give back.** I strongly believe that it is important to be appreciative of the gifts in your life, and to help others. There are lots of ways to do this. Choose those that appeal most to you. Start now. I began donating ten percent of my income to worthwhile causes when I was still in graduate school. Grad students don't earn much—but by starting then, it eliminated the excuse that there isn't enough. There's always enough—in fact, I've personally found that this is a key to success. The more I donate (in terms of time and money), the more successful I am.

These eight principles provide a wonderful foundation for true leadership. Applying each of them can—and will—lead to extraordinary results.

# # #

Dr. Audri G. Lanford has been the founder and CEO of three very different businesses: Micro Dynamics, Ltd., one of the fastest growing private companies in the United States, an Inc. 500 company; NETrageous Inc., the oldest and largest direct results Internet marketing company; and now WZ.com, the #1 on-line company connecting busy people with what they love to do, with more than 750,000 subscribers. She has helped thousands of small- and medium-sized companies use the Internet profitably. Audri has been featured in hundreds of print and Web publications, including *Forbes, BusinessWeek,* the *Wall Street Journal, Wired* magazine, and *InfoWorld.*

Section VII

Live Your Priorities!

Live Your Priorities!

Joan Eleanor Gustafson

Stephen Covey, author of *The 7 Habits of Highly Effective People*, explains that we spend time in one of four ways and that there are two factors that define an activity. These two factors are *urgent* and *important*.

Urgent items require immediate attention, such as a ringing telephone. Urgent matters are usually visible and popular with others, and they are usually pleasant, easy, and fun to do. However, they are not necessarily a priority and are most often unimportant.

Important items relate to results. If something is important, it contributes to one's mission, values, and/or high-priority goals. Important matters usually require a person to be proactive. If we don't have a clear idea of what is important in our lives, we will often react to the urgent matters and ignore or dismiss those that are important.

According to Covey's model, we spend our time in the following four ways:

1. Activities that are urgent and important, e.g., deadline-driven projects
2. Activities that are important but not urgent, e.g., relationship building, planning
3. Activities that are urgent but not important, e.g., interruptions
4. Activities that are not urgent and not important, e.g., trivia

Most adults spend most of their time doing things that are urgent, regardless of whether these things are important. The most effective leaders spend most of their time on activities that are important and not urgent.

When I interviewed Jill Lublin, international speaker and author of *Guerrilla Publicity*, she said that her top priorities are to grow as a person, to serve others, and to be successful. To Jill, her idea of success is to be a live role model for others, as well as to be successful in her business. Her family and friends know that she is there for them when they need her, and she makes it a priority to be there physically, emotionally, mentally, spiritually, and financially. Another of Jill's priorities is to take time for herself. She calls this time her "Jill time," and she schedules time for herself every week.

Our priorities are based on our values. When I discussed values with Linda Chandler, who gives keynote speeches and seminars on leadership, she brought up the subject of materialism. "So many people think that materialistic solutions will make them feel better, that it will salve the wounds and boost their egos, but that is not what really happens," she said. "Materialism will go only so far. Yes, there are people who will live their lives for material success, and it may seem that they are successful; however, we don't see the inside of other people's lives." She added that her experience in working with some of these people is that those who concentrate on materialism alone, sacrificing other would-be priorities in their lives, do not really feel successful.

Linda also stated, "You can be very happy being rich, but success is about balancing. It's about blending all areas of your life—family, friends, country, associations, emotions, and spirituality."

Jill Lublin and Linda Chandler are two women who know their priorities and live those priorities, as do all of the women who contributed to this book.

Eleanor Roosevelt was another leader who knew and lived her priorities. When her husband, Franklin D. Roosevelt, was stricken with poliomyelitis, she attended to him devotedly. To keep his interest in politics alive, she became active in the women's division of the State Democratic Committee. As he served as governor of New York and later as president of the United States, she dedicated her life to his purposes. She was a major voice in his administration, promoting programs to aid racial minorities, the disenfranchised, and the underprivileged. After her husband's death, she continued to live her priorities, serving as an American delegate to the United Nations General Assembly. Her great sensitivity to the underprivileged and her constant work to improve their situation made her one of the most loved women of her generation.

# # #

Some leaders are definitely born women, and all women can be leaders if they desire to be leaders. As leaders, we each develop our own style. This makes each of us unique and helps to create synergy in the world.

All of the female leaders featured in this book recognize the importance of learning, of persistence, and of hard work. They all dare to dream, grow through challenge, set powerful goals, focus on the power and possibilities in people, set high standards and live accordingly, communicate effectively, and live their priorities.

My promise to you is that, by integrating and incorporating the recommendations and action steps from this book, you will enhance your success as a leader.

Appendix A

Leadership Checklist

Use the following checklist for increasing your leadership skills. Start by marking an "x" in the boxes preceding the items that you already do. Then circle the items that are your next priorities, and start working on them.

Effective female leaders . . .

❑ Dare to dream; are visionaries
❑ Show passion for the vision
❑ Use intuitive as well as analytical skills

❑ Challenge processes and the "status quo"
❑ Seek challenges
❑ Look for ways to innovate
❑ Embrace change
❑ Establish a sense of urgency
❑ Create short-term wins
❑ Are excited about the future

❏ Set clear goals and milestones

❏ Focus on the power and possibilities of people
❏ Surround themselves with excellent people
❏ Generate excitement and enthusiasm
❏ Create synergy
❏ Align people behind the vision and strategies; inspire a shared vision
❏ Develop cooperative relationships and partnerships
❏ Expect the best from people
❏ Delegate authority along with responsibility
❏ Contribute to the success of others
❏ Recognize others for their contributions
❏ Treat others with respect

❏ Communicate effectively
❏ Clearly articulate thoughts, ideas, and vision
❏ Understand, appreciate, and translate the inarticulate ideas of others

❏ Set high standards and live accordingly
❏ Set an example; model behavior

❏ Live their priorities

Appendix B

Biographies of Other Contributors

Linda Chandler

Linda Chandler, former senior vice president of Sutro & Company, was one of the youngest persons and the first woman to become vice president of a major U.S. securities firm. She went on to co-found and serve as CEO/president of America's first all-women securities firm.

Linda is a nationally recognized authority on capital formation, financial structuring and fast growth business strategies. She has written two books, including *Winning Strategies for Capital Formation* published by McGraw-Hill. Linda has also authored and produced five best-selling business audio albums, and is an international keynote speaker. She has been featured in many publications, including *Money* magazine, *Inc.* magazine, and *Success*.

A member of Phi Delta Theta Scholastic Honor Society, Linda holds bachelor's and master's degrees from Iowa State University. She addressed the United Nations at age seventeen as a United Nations scholarship winner. Linda has been honored in *Who's Who in the West*, *Who's Who of American Women*, and *Who's Who in Finance & Industry*. She is managing partner/chief executive officer of Chandler-Drew, LLC, a private equity investments and mergers and acquisition consultancy.

Leslie Dashew

Leslie Dashew is president of Human Side of Enterprise, an organizational development firm, and a partner in the Aspen Family Business Group. She has combined her thirty-year background in organizational development and family therapy to specialize in consultation to family business, as well as other private and public organizations.

As an author, trusted advisor, speaker and consultant, Leslie seeks to help her clients appreciate and fully utilize their talents and resources as well as those of the people whose lives they touch. She is the author of *The Best of the Human Side*, and co-author of *Working with Family Businesses: A Guide for Professionals.* She also publishes a periodic newsletter and is quoted often in professional periodicals.

Jill Lublin

Jill Lublin is a nationally renowned public relations strategist and marketing expert. As the CEO of the public relations consulting firm, Promising Promotion, Jill creates successful public relations strategies and techniques that implement bottom line results. Twenty-years of experience working with ABC, NBC, CBS, and other national media has given her great insight into what works for the media.

Jill has completed a training video and two audiotapes, *7 Key Points to Powerful Publicity* and *Insider's Edge to Powerful Publicity*. She is the author of the soon to be best-seller, *Guerrilla Publicity* (Adams Media), part of the best-selling Jay Levinson *Guerrilla Marketing* Series. In addition, Jill is the founder of GoodNews Media, Inc., and host of the nationally syndicated radio show, "Do the Dream."

Appendix C

Recommended Reading

Bennis, Warren. *On Becoming a Leader*. Cambridge, Mass.: Perseus Publishing, 1994.

Benton, Debra A. *How to Act Like a CEO: 10 Rules for Getting to the Top and Staying There*. New York, N.Y.: McGraw-Hill, 2001.

Carnegie, Dale, Levine, Stuart R., and Crom, Michael A. *The Leader in You: How to Win Friends, Influence People and Succeed in a Changing World*. Pocket Books, 1993.

Covey, Stephen R. *Principle-Centered Leadership*. New York, N.Y.: Simon & Schuster, 1992.

Deaton, Dennis R. *The Book on Mind Management*. Mesa, Ariz.: MMI Publishing, 1994.

Dilenschneider, Robert L. *A Briefing for Leaders: Communication As the Ultimate Exercise of Power*. New York, N.Y.: HarperCollins Publishers, 1992.

Down, Colleen. *It Takes a Mother to Raise a Village*. Draper, Utah: Lightwave Publications, 2001.

Gustafson, Joan Eleanor. *A Woman Can Do That! 10 Strategies for Creating Success in Your Life*. Phoenix, Ariz.: Leader Dynamics, 2001.

Gustafson, Joan Eleanor and Lanford, Audri, Ph.D. *How to Control Your Destiny through Your Attitude*. Available in e-book format at wz.com.

Hesselbein, Frances, et al. *The Leader of the Future: New Visions, Strategies, and Practices for the Next Era (The Drucker Foundation Future Series)*. San Francisco, Calif.: Josey Bass Publishers, 1997.

Kouzes, James M. and Posner, Barry Z. *The Leadership Challenge: How to Keep Getting Extraordinary Things Done in Organizations*. San Francisco, Calif.: Josey Bass Publishers, 1995.

Hollands, Jean. *Same Game Different Rules: How to Get Ahead Without Being a Bully Broad, Ice Queen, or "Ms. Understood."* New York: McGraw Hill College Division, 2001.

Nanus, Burt. *Visionary Leadership*. San Francisco, Calif.: Josey Bass Publishers, 1992.

Peale, Norman Vincent. *The Power of Positive Thinking*. Englewood Cliffs, N.J.: Prentice-Hall, Inc., 1987.

Stevens, Bobbie. *Unlimited Futures: How to Understand the Life You Have and Create the Life You Want*. Naples, Fla.: Tara Publishing, 2001.

Tichy, Noel M. *The Leadership Engine: How Winning Companies Build Leaders at Every Level*. New York, N.Y.: HarperCollins Publishers, 1997.

Index

excellence, 107
expectations of others, 110, 148–49
experimentation, 34

F
failures, learning from, 34–35, 182
fairness, 163
faith, 145
fear, 78, 115
female leaders, 28–30. *See also*
    leaders
feminine skills, 184
flexibility, 94, 114, 164
"flight or fight" response, 169
focus, 54–56, 78, 81, 115, 157, 161,
    197
Forbes, 192
Fort Yuma Indian Hospital, 163
Fortune, 48
Fortune 500 companies, 65
Franchise Acquisition Corporation,
    55
friendships, 122–24
fulfillment, 111, 137
fun, 14, 87, 119, 124, 167, 190
future orientation, 5

G
Gans, Dr. Steven, 70
Gardner, John, 44
gender roles, 169–70
Genetronics, Inc., 63
Gifts of the Spirit, 120
giving back, 77, 171, 191
goals
    achieving, 55, 92–94, 98, 164
    setting, 21, 24, 78, 83–84, 91–94,
        103, 197
Golden Nuggets, 177
Goodman, Barbara, 4, 11–15
Goodman, Dan, 11–15
Goodman, Lisa, 12, 14
Goodman, Lori, 12, 14
Growth and Leadership Center
    (GLC), 170

Guerrilla Publicity, 175, 196
Gustafson, Joan, 96

H
happiness, 119
Harker, Victoria, 33, 39–43
health, 26, 56–57, 59, 98, 118–20,
    122–23
helping others, 56, 69, 77, 86, 111,
    171
Herold Enterprises, 172
Herold, Linda, 155, 171–72
Herold Report, The, 172
Hersey, John, 108–9
Hesburgh, Father Theodore, 4
high achievers, 72–74
Hill, Lister, 37
Hofmann, Lois Joy Crandell, 38,
    61–63
Hollands, Jean, 155, 169–70
honesty, 175, 176, 190
Hospice, 122, 163
How to Act Like a CEO, 168
How to Think Like a CEO, 168
HSBC Investment Bank, 49
humor, 114, 166–68

I
IBM, 135
ideality, 5
identity, 171–72, 184–85
imagery, 5
imagination, 5
important activities, 195
Inc., 55
indecisiveness, 52
influence, 114
informality, 35
InfoWorld, 192
innovation, 33–34, 38
inspiring others, 111, 133, 177
integrity, 175–77, 190
Intellectual Asset Consulting, 182
Internet World's Deconstructing, 66
intuition, 13, 14, 36, 42, 58, 114

V

values, 25, 80–82, 119, 180, 196
Van Derzee, Carrie, 124
Vernon, Lillian, 38, 50–52
visionaries, 4–5, 17, 29
visionary leadership, 17–18
Visionary Leadership, 108
visionary thinking, 16–19
visions, 5, 18, 25–27, 50, 55, 107–
    8, 114, 126–28, 164
visualization, 5–8, 21, 56, 78, 93,
    102–3, 185
volunteerism, 134, 142

W

Wall Street Journal, 192
Washington, George, 128
West, Donna, 122
Whitman, Meg, 40
Wilson, Woodrow, 9
Wired, 192
wisdom, 114, 115
Wolf, Connie, 110, 147–48
Woman Can Do That!, A, 96
Woodruff, Bob, 112
Wright, Sylvia, 69
WZ.com, 190, 191

Y

yoga, 26, 28, 185

About Joan Eleanor Gustafson

Joan Eleanor Gustafson, founder and president of Success and Leadership Dynamics, is an international professional speaker and consultant. She has coached hundreds of individuals in achieving their desired results, both in their careers and in their personal lives. In her consulting practice, she specializes in maximizing business results through effective leadership, individual growth and development, and team building.

Prior to founding Success and Leadership Dynamics, Joan was a member of the corporate marketing management committee at 3M, where she held international leadership and management positions for twenty-six years. In these positions, her responsibilities included the areas of e-business, customer satisfaction, knowledge management, communications, strategic outsourcing, sales and marketing productivity improvement, and information technology. Her international responsibility included a two-year assignment in Europe, where she lived in Paris, France, and maintained an office in Brussels, Belgium, as well as in Paris.

Joan holds a bachelor of arts degree in business management and an MBA in management. She is a member of National Speakers Association and International Coach Federation and is president elect of the Phoenix Chapter of Professional Coaches and Mentors Association. She is on the faculty of the University of Phoenix, where she teaches graduate level courses in international management and e-business.

As a professional speaker, Joan has spoken to business and professional audiences throughout the United States, Europe, Canada, and Asia. She is the author of *A Woman Can Do That! 10 Strategies for Creating Success in Your Life*.

Joan and her husband, Cliff, live in Anthem, Arizona. She has two grown children, Bryan and Shelley, and is the proud grandmother of Alea, Ethan, and Erika.

Quick Order Form

Fax orders: (623) 551-3858. Copy and send this form.

Telephone toll-free: 1-877-824-3014. Have your credit card ready.

E-mail orders: orders@leaderdynamics.com

Postal Orders: Leader Dynamics, Joan Gustafson
PMB 296, 3655 W. Anthem Way, Suite A109
Anthem, AZ 85086, USA.
Telephone: (623) 551-3881
Please send me *Some Leaders Are Born Women!*

_____ copies (paper back) @ $14.95 =   _____
_____ copies (hard cover) @ $19.95 =   _____
Arizona residents, add 7.2% sales tax   _____

Shipping:
U.S: $4.00 for the first book and $2.00 for each additional book
International: $9.00 for the first book, $5.00 each additional book   _____

Grand Total for Order: _____

Name: _____

Address: _____

City: _____ State: _____ ZIP: _____

Country (if other than USA): _____

Telephone: _____ E-mail address: _____
Payment: __ Check __ Credit card: __ Visa __ MasterCard __ Am. Express

Card number: _____ Exp. Date: _____

Signature: _____

Please also send information on the following:
_____ Executive and Leadership Coaching
_____ Organizational Consulting
_____ Keynote Speeches by Joan Gustafson
_____ Speaker Coaching